MAKE
WORLDS

Lia Schulz

Transform Your Life

10 Steps To Release What Doesn't Serve You And Build The Life You Truly Want

© 2023 **Europe Books** | London
www.europebooks.co.uk | info@europebooks.co.uk

ISBN 9791220142922
First edition: September 2023

Transform Your Life

10 Steps To Release What Doesn't Serve You
And Build The Life You Truly Want

To my son, Sebastian.
The light of my life.

Introduction

- Have you ever been in a difficult place and found yourself looking for a solution to depression, anxiety, or any other challenging life situation?
- How often have you felt so frustrated you wished you could escape your reality and start over?
- How many times have you been through difficult times that made everything seem dark and hopeless, and you struggled to muster the motivation to move forward?
- How often have you sought a solution to depression, anxiety, or life challenges in self-help books and inspirational gurus, only to find that the proffered solution is usually in a two-to-four-word sentence, usually along the lines of *Let it go, be positive, or you have the power.*

Like most people, you have probably been through a fair amount of life challenges and can relate to these questions and the scenario they paint.

Now, while *"let it go, be positive, you have the power"* and all such things are wonderful sentiments, do you truly understand what these concepts mean? More importantly, have you implemented them into your life? If you haven't, you are not alone.

Like you, I was once looking for answers to personal challenges. You see: I had been depressed for almost two years and battling severe social anxiety.

Things were so bad that, in two years, I had lost most of my friends, two jobs because of bullying, and my two grandmothers died while I was living abroad. I had relationship problems with my mother and had lost a baby at week eight of pregnancy. I was devastated and didn't know how to move forward.

For more than a year, I tried looking for ways to fix my social anxiety, but without much success, unfortunately, especially because being abroad in a country where I lacked my usual familiar social contact made things incredibly challenging.

However, I was determined to find a solution, a fix, or anything that would work.

I read every social anxiety book I could lay my hands on, started meditation, exercised regularly, and interacted with strangers and other people (to my discomfort), but nothing seemed to work for me.

For such a long time, it seemed like the moment I made some progress, something new would come into my life to shake everything again. And with each new disappointment, my depression grew deeper while my anxiety worsened.

I kept reading all the self-help books I could find and buy, watched thousands of motivational YouTube videos, and experimented with many healing techniques: journaling, meditation, healthy eating, exercise, yoga, CBT Therapy, EFT Tapping, and many others.

Unfortunately, although all these tools are great, none of them was really working for me. I needed a plan, but because I didn't understand how to implement these concepts, I often felt worse because I couldn't see massive changes after implementing them.

Right now, we live in a society that pushes us to our limits and motivates us to be attractive, productive, successful, hard-working, and rich by age 30 to fit social standards because it seems every influential person is doing that.

But that is not the truth for most people, something I learned much later. That was not the case for me, and because of not living up to these social standards, I sunk deeper and deeper into depression, and anxiety took hold.

Fortunately, I never gave up on myself.

After a long, deep journey of self-discovery, I realized that the secret to achieving success and building the life we truly want doesn't lie in a productivity routine or how many income streams we have.

Fundamentally, living our dream life is about reaching our highest potential by knowing exactly who we are and releasing everything that is not serving us.

Doing this is the rudimental step to growth because when we are sure of who we are, we know exactly what we want and can work towards achieving our goals. We are also happier, more emotionally stable, and physically healthier, which gives us the motivation and focus we need to build the life we want.

To transform my life and release anxiety and depression, I learned that I had to focus on finding and healing the root cause of my mental health issues.

I hadn't realized it at the time, but I was carrying a heavy burden from my past: traumatic events that happened in my childhood, feelings of guilt and shame, and grief that I hadn't overcome. All those trapped emotions were causing me to feel unworthy and not good enough, which led to low self-esteem and social anxiety.

When I started healing my past and releasing all the negative emotions, traumatic experiences and limiting beliefs about myself and the world, I started rediscovering myself and valuing myself more. With increased self-esteem, my social anxiety and depression also started improving.

In this book, I want to show you the steps I followed in the course of four years to recover from depression and anxiety and completely transform my life.

It took me a long time to gather and put together all the transformational concepts in this book into an easy, step-by-step program covering specific actions you can take to release everything that doesn't serve you, including traumas, unresolved emotions, toxic relationships, and negative habits, and start building a stable foundation for your new life.

This guidebook is not just for anyone suffering from depression and anxiety or only ideal for people dealing with many life difficulties. This book is for everyone who wants to improve their overall health and lifestyle, release negativity, get to know themselves better, improve their relationships, and learn how to live a happier and more fulfilled life.

If you are ready to start living a happier, more fulfilled, and more abundant life, let's dive in!

Part 1: How to Start

Welcome to your healing journey of self-discovery and transformation.

Like any other journey, the most important and difficult thing to do is start. It takes a lot of energy to begin something new, and the process also involves a lot of fear.

Our ego has one purpose: to protect us from adversity and keep us safe. Unfortunately, that also means it normally sees every new situation as a potential threat. So there is often an inclination to delay or postpone new projects because of fear. We are either afraid of success, feel we don't have the resources to complete it (time, money, or knowledge), or lack the motivation or desire to change.

However, since you want something to change in your life, which is why you are reading this book, you need to start small, without expectation. Just start!

In this section, I will share my story to give you some inspiration. I haven't had the worst life, but it has been a very difficult one, with many challenges to overcome.

If you're wondering why I would open up to you and share my most painful experiences and deepest pain, it is because I know that hearing what I have gone through can help you realize that no matter how your life situation is right now, you can always change it. There is nothing you cannot overcome if you set your mind to it.

My goal is not to trigger you, shock you or make you feel sorry for me. The aim is to make you aware that all those tools, techniques, and advice I give you were not only learned in theory but were also part of my healing experience.

After overcoming grief, loss, and negative emotions, I can assure you that everything I share truly works, and although we are all different, I am certain that at least some of the techniques, if not all, will help you heal yourself as well.

I would also like to push you to start by giving you some tips and questions you can ask yourself to find the motivation that will keep you going. We can easily make things happen when we commit to changing, improving, and healing.

Finally, in the last chapter of this section, you will find a summary of what you can expect from this journey, my recommendation on how to read and utilize the book as a healing tool, discovery journey, or self-development guide, and the outcomes that are waiting for you at the end if you open yourself up and follow the guidance step by step.

And remember, you can come back to any of the steps later in life when facing negative emotions, difficult relationships, bad habits, or any other event that threatens to disrupt harmony in your life. They are all timeless tools that can help you let go and move forward with your life.

My Story

I would like to start by telling you a little bit more about my life story and the struggles I had growing up, so you can understand the turning point in my life that made me seek change and take these steps to build a new life.

2018 was the most difficult year of my life. I had changed jobs the year before because the company I was working for was financially unstable, and a colleague of mine was emotionally abusive towards me.

Before the change, I was a happy, energetic person who enjoyed life, a job, and relationships. But when the bullying started, it completely broke me down. The humiliation and pain from the abuse deeply hurt me and drained my energy to the point that I was feeling sick and burnt out.

As a consequence of this experience, I developed social anxiety. Until now, social anxiety has been my second biggest battle. It started subtly and gradually became a monster that took over my thoughts and behavior. It reached a point where I couldn't look people in the eye, felt nervous around colleagues and even friends, and the thought of being rejected because of my anxiety made the spiral even worse.

However, I wasn't really aware of what was happening at the time. I knew I was dealing with anxiety, but being such a sociable and communicative person, I couldn't understand why I felt so anxious around others. I thought it was just a side effect of the abuse and that it would disappear, so I decided to start a new job instead of healing my anxiety first.

The new job seemed perfect; it was a start-up with young colleagues that seemed very cool. There was a game of mini soccer in the office and a dart tournament. I quickly got along with my colleagues and felt comfortable there, but my manager was a very difficult person. You could see how hurt he was, and he used to put people down and snap at us at meetings if we said something he didn't like. He especially hated me.

It was an absolute nightmare working for him. He would ridicule me, ignore me, give me very difficult tasks, or sometimes no tasks at all. We shared the same desk, and he constantly looked at everything I was doing. I now realize he wanted me to go, but I was so naive at the time and had so little self-love that I allowed the abuse. Due to the constant criticism, my social anxiety got worse, and I started to fall into depression and was terrified at the idea of looking for another job.

As the days went by, the bullying got even worse. This person started to involve some of my other colleagues and spread lies about me so they would laugh at me, ridicule me and humiliate me. It was like the previous experience I had, but even worse.

Even colleagues I thought were my friends and for whom I had high esteem got involved, and it was very painful to see people around me believe those things and ridicule me because of it.

Some even went as far as pretending they were still my friends to gather information against me. Others went to my desk to make fun of me during my most difficult moments. In the midst of that experience, my grandmother died.

In 2014, I moved to Germany because my husband is German, and we decided to get married and start our lives here. Although I often visited my family in Mexico, I hadn't seen my grandmother in over a year. She was one of the most important people in my life, like a second mother to me, and her passing brought great grief and pain. It also brought to the surface some issues my mother and I hadn't resolved, and our relationship started to suffer from it.

This all happened in April, the month the abuse at work got worse. I was devastated and depressed, grieving my grandmother, and my relationship with my mother. My life was completely crumbling down.

I have blurry memories of those months because I was in survival mode. I couldn't eat or sleep, and my body was shutting down. I didn't have the energy to defend myself or do something about it and didn't have much support except for my husband, who also didn't know what to do. I reached a point where I didn't want to live anymore. I felt alone, lost in life, and deeply hurt.

I got my first job when I was 17, and working became my everything. I knew I couldn't return to those job types, but I didn't know what else to do. Needless to say, my social anxiety was at its worse. I could barely talk to people without a panic attack, which kept me from meeting new friends or creating better connections.

During those critical days, I found out I was pregnant. My husband and I had been trying to start a family some months before this experience, but I am still amazed that my body could get pregnant after all the stress I was living under. The news of a new baby gave me hope and was the light that helped me go through that darkness.

However, we lost our baby at around eight weeks pregnant. I couldn't believe it, another catastrophe yet again. The pain was so strong I became numb. I was completely lost, with severe anxiety and deeply depressed. That was the darkest moment of my life. And that was my year: 2018. I will never forget this year because it completely broke me down. It cracked me open. Everything around me was falling apart, and I had no idea how to change it.

During those dark moments, I did the last thing I could: I reached out to God, the universe, or whatever you call the life force that created all of us. I had no choice but to surrender my situation to a higher power, even though I didn't believe in anything spiritual back then. But I couldn't take it anymore.

I had always been strong, someone who would do everything I could to change my situation. After surrendering my situation to something higher than me, I immediately felt I couldn't defeat myself and others by giving up: there had to be a purpose to all my life experiences. And that is when my journey began.

My healing journey was not an easy one. I realized I had suppressed many memories and traumatic experiences from my childhood, and they were all coming out to my conscious mind concurrently.

I recognized the deep grief I still had after my father's death when I was 23. I found out he was sick very unexpectedly, and he passed away a couple of weeks later. Since I am the oldest sibling, I needed to take care of the paperwork and other things after his passing, so I never truly took time to heal.

I also identified that I hadn't moved on from the loss of my two grandmothers. I felt guilty for not being with them when they passed and not managing to attend their funeral because of the distance. They were also one of the few close family members I had left. Unfortunately, it did not stop there.

The deep pain I lived as a child when my aunt and cousins passed in a tragic accident also came to the surface. I was so young that I had completely suppressed that memory and never healed that wound. And that's not all, a deep grief arose from having lost so many family members, like my grandfather and uncle -and also some friends - during my childhood years.

Then the abandonment I felt when my parents got divorced resurfaced. Their divorce happened when I was eleven, and I had to be my mom's emotional support and the intermediary between my parents. From this young age, I took on a lot of responsibility at home.

A couple of years after that, my mom, siblings, and I moved to another city where we didn't have any family to support us, and my mom worked a lot, so I took on even more responsibilities around the house. I used to cook, clean the house, care for my siblings and help coordinate their after-school activities. I was 13 then, and the responsibility placed on my shoulders at such a young age was too much to handle.

All this pressure and responsibility led me to develop an eating disorder. At the time, I felt it was because I wanted to be thinner and didn't like my body. In retrospect, I now understand that it was my way to have "control" over something since I couldn't control the world around me.

The battle with my eating disorder lasted several years and deeply impacted my self-image and self-esteem. During stable periods of my life, the eating disorder was not as pronounced, and I used exercise to process emotions and feel better about myself.

However, when I faced difficulties, it would aggravate. After some experiences with emotional abuse, things got worse.

When I was 16, my mom's boyfriend moved in with us. My mom and his boyfriend had been dating for a couple of years, and he seemed like such a nice person. It seemed like he was deeply in love with my mom and enjoyed being with us as a new family. It wasn't until he moved in with us that we started noticing toxic and abusive behavior. He wanted to control everything we did, didn't allow us to see friends or go out of the house after school, and was a compulsive liar.

He enjoyed playing us against each other and said hurtful things to us to make us feel bad about ourselves. My mom was still working a lot, so she didn't truly see the emotional abuse we were suffering at her boyfriend's hands. It took her some years to realize that everything he said to her about us was a lie and that we were suffering from narcissistic abuse.

The years he lived with us felt like a prison to me. My self-esteem suffered a lot. I created a very distorted self-image, and my eating disorder worsened. The resulting feelings of unworthiness I developed led me to believe I was not good enough. It made me seek validation from others and allow abuse from others as well.

In the chapter on how to clean addictions and addictive behaviors in the next part of the book, I'll share my experience on how I overcame the eating disorder.

Addiction can relate to substance abuse and all our compulsive behaviors. In my case, it was an eating disorder; for you, it can be shopping, eating, or negative thinking.

In that chapter, I explain how they relate to feelings of unworthiness and negative emotions we haven't processed and share tools that can help you overcome them.

The lack of boundaries and self-love also led me to attract toxic relationships. I sometimes found myself in relationships with people who didn't respect me and made me feel bad, unworthy, and guilty. And the worst part is that I always blamed myself.

I will dedicate a chapter of this book to talking about how to manage difficult or toxic relationships and how this can dramatically improve your well-being and your approach toward life. Since I know walking away from relationships can be extremely difficult, especially for people who suffer from codependency, like I did, I think reading my guide and the lessons I learned can help you evaluate the kind of people around you and the kind of people you want to have in your life.

In summary, all those suppressed memories started to come out to my conscious mind one by one at that time. All my past was resurfacing, asking me to heal the open wounds I had walked around with for many years that had kept me stuck.

My wake-up call was the baby I lost because it changed my perspective in life and made me realize that the one I had been building was not stable. It helped me realize that I kept repeating the same patterns and something needed to change if I were to improve my life and well-being.

I started reading psychology, personal development, and spiritual books and tried to gather as much knowledge as possible to improve my situation. I also started meditating, journaling, exercising regularly, and paying attention to my health and what I was putting in my body.

After some months, my health started to improve, my self-esteem recovered a little, and I began to feel better. I no longer had intrusive thoughts and had gained a new love for life. I woke up, finally took responsibility for myself and my life, and stopped making excuses. That is when I finally faced my situation, all the past trauma, and repressed feelings. When I grieved my grandparents, my father, my uncle, my aunt, and my cousins and let myself feel the pain, the guilt, and shame. I let it all go.

After intensive work that involved trying all the methods available, hearing amazing advice, and applying powerful tools presented by great inspirational teachers, I turned my life around.

In retrospect, I have to say that the path has not been easy, but I am proud to say that my life has completely transformed. My health has never been better, my relationships are stronger, I have a job that I love and I have developed unshakable inner peace and unconditional love for myself. And above all, I truly enjoy my life.

Why I Wrote this Book

I wrote this book because the beginning of my journey was not easy, and it was extremely difficult to understand some of the concepts I read and put into practice. I realized that it is not so easy to "let go" and that I didn't even know how to start or what to do. I'd heard the words "let go" and "release what doesn't serve you" so often that I got very stressed when I didn't know how to do it and when the things I tried didn't work.

Ultimately, it took me a lot of time to figure out what all the concepts meant. I also discovered that healing is a process or a journey that plays out in layers. Truly healing from a situation takes time and patience; the process is impossible to hurry along.

Retrospectively, I have realized that there were things I could have done better to accelerate the healing process and stop going back to the same patterns. I also spent a lot of time reading all the books I could find on the topic, many of which have repeated concepts and techniques.

For this reason, in this book, I want to share what I learned and experienced so that you don't have to spend years figuring out how to heal. It took me several years to understand and apply the concepts that helped me heal, but they really transformed my life when I did.

I wrote this book to help others have an easier healing and transformation journey. Thus, this book is a collection of all the knowledge I have acquired after a lot of research and practical experience with letting go of what doesn't serve me, thereby transforming my life.

I have done my utmost best to create an easy-to-follow guideline full of the best practices and proven steps you can take to overcome any difficult situation you might be facing.

I promise that if you integrate the various strategies and ideas discussed in this guidebook, you can easily overcome depression and anxiety, release the negative emotions from your past experiences and let go of everything that doesn't serve you. When you know yourself better, you will find your path and start building the life you want, as I did.

How To Get Started

I woke up one day hating my life. I wasn't motivated to get up and didn't really see the point of continuing to live. I had quit my job and was dealing with severe social anxiety and depression. Some of my friends had betrayed me, and my marriage was starting to suffer the consequences of stress, constant irritation, and unhappiness. I felt completely alone. This was the deepest point in my depression. I was only focusing on what I didn't have and was frustrated with how everything had turned out.

From a very young age, I always felt it was my destiny to succeed in my professional life; thus, being unemployed felt like a major failure. I felt a deep need to prove myself and fulfill all external expectations from others, which made it more difficult to accept my situation.

At the time, I thought success meant having a good job, earning money, and going up the corporate ladder. Although that is a form of success for many people, it is not for me anymore.

After a period of feeling sorry for myself, complaining about my situation, and blaming everyone for what they had done to me or not done for me, I decided to change. I couldn't take it anymore. I knew I was a strong person, which meant giving up was not a choice.

My dad was a big motivator. Even though he was not there in person to cheer me up, I knew he would not have wanted me to give up without a fight. As horrible as my situation seemed back then, it would never be as bad as losing someone you love. So, if I had already dealt with my father's death, which was the most difficult thing I have ever faced, I knew I had the strength to change my reality.

That is when I decided to start my healing journey. Starting is the most difficult step of the guideline and of any change we face in life.

Starting something new as adults can be a struggle, especially if we think too much about it and let our insecurities, fears, and worries take over our brains at that moment.

For example, going to the gym the first time can be scary; starting a new class can be frightening. This normally happens because we don't know what to expect and want to stay in control.

When starting something new, our body and mind also need extra energy and focus, which makes us reticent to begin. But once you conquer the fear and start moving forward, you will get used to your new circumstances and gain momentum. And then, the process becomes easier.

Something that works for me is not to think too much about it, especially if what I am starting is something that will benefit me or enhance my life. The more you think about starting something new, the more your mind will figure out a reason why you shouldn't, which is our ego protecting ourselves. In any case, the real force that makes you start is determining why you don't want to be in the same situation anymore, visualizing what you want to achieve, and having a significant motivator.

When I was in a toxic relationship at 22, it took me a while to realize that the relationship was abusive and was harming me on an emotional level. However, after months of feeling insecure and hurt, I hit rock bottom. It was my birthday, and my boyfriend didn't even text to say, "Happy Birthday." He didn't even care and probably forgot (or did it to hurt me even more).

That same birthday, another person I had met recently called me at midnight to be the first to congratulate me, then later sent me a bouquet. He was just my friend, but it made me realize that there were people who cared about me. It also showed me how I wasn't valuing myself enough because I was allowing an abusive person in my life. That day, I made up my mind and terminated the relationship for good. It takes a consciousness shift to realize that something in our lives is not working anymore and to find the strength and motivation to start the change and growth process.

To make starting easier for you, I have some questions you can ask yourself at the beginning of this journey. In the example below, I show you what I asked myself and my answers.

Think about that thing you want to change in your life and the reason why you are reading this book, and answer the following questions.

1. Why do I want to start/change_____?
I want to overcome depression and anxiety and enjoy life again.

2. What is my motivation? Why do I really want things to be different?
I am longing for deep close connections and friendships. I am happiest when I'm around other people who love me and respect me for who I am.

3. How do I want things to be in the future? What is my goal?
I want to be happy, enjoy life, build fulfilling relationships and be a good example for the people around me. I want to attract better experiences in my life and gain inner peace.

4. *How would my life be if I started/changed____?*
If I didn't have social anxiety, I would have many friends; I would get along with more people and be more open to new experiences.

Answer the questions as detailed as you want and try to visualize how your life would be after the change you want to make. Feel what you would feel if the change were real. If you don't think your motivator is powerful enough, keep digging by asking the same question with your answer. For example:

Why do I want to enjoy life? Why do I want to be there for my family?

Keep asking yourself deeper questions until you understand your deepest reasons and feel like it is enough motivation for you. If you are still hesitant, don't worry, you can return to this part later and start over, and maybe you'll find your motivator after you start seeing some changes.

The most important thing here is your willingness to change and to start.

I began my transformation journey four years ago. In the middle of my depression, I decided I didn't want that life anymore. I wanted to strengthen my relationships, especially my marriage. I wanted to create a life I enjoyed living, and feel content and at peace.

However, there were a few things I was not ready to let go of. I knew my job at the time was not fulfilling and that my calling was in another area, but I didn't want to let go of the security of a corporate job. So, I looked for a similar one, and a similar thing happened. Things started changing for me after I surrendered to the idea that

I was not meant for that specific type of job because of misalignment with my personality and skills. That was when my real transformation began.

In order to change something in our lives, there are things and situations we need to let go of, even if it is scary. But it is never in vain: we only open up space for new things to come.

Therefore, be ready to start, be willing to change and let go, and begin this journey with an open mind. In the end, I can promise you that your life won't look the same.

What You Can Expect

If you are like me, you probably want to know what you can expect from your transformation journey, how long it might take, and what you can accomplish.

Let me be honest: it all depends on the depth of your current situation, how passionate you are about the change, and how much inner work you are willing to do.

The first part of the transformation journey is to let go. This part of the journey involves letting go of everything that no longer serves you. It took me months to realize what that meant, which is why, in this book, I have broken it down for you into different focus areas and steps you can follow.

Letting go is a very abstract subject. However, after a long trial and error process with my situation, I finally figured out the best way to start letting go of things, people, experiences, feelings, habits, and everything in your life that doesn't serve you anymore and is holding you back.

The order is important because it is easier to let go of material possessions than relationships or thought patterns. With every step, you will gain more confidence in the release process and have more tools you can use as you continue your healing journey.

When you let go of clutter, you will have more time and space to enjoy time with people you love. When you let go of negative relationships, you allow yourself time to heal your emotional wounds and get to know yourself better. When you know yourself, it is easier to overwrite negative habits or behavior patterns and change your negative self-talk.

This part of the process will take the longest, and you should prepare to dive deep and get excited for the things you will learn about yourself and your life in general.

After the letting go process, I can assure you that you will see a dramatic transformation in your life. You will feel lighter and ready to start a new life without being weighed down by unnecessary past baggage.

The second part of your transformation is about building strong foundations to create the life you want. In this part of the book, we will go through the same areas covered by part one but backward and focus on changing your thought patterns and finding out what matters most.

Then we will focus on working on your feelings and emotions. The tools I will show you here are ways to be more in touch with your emotions and gain excellent coping skills to react better to the different situations you may face in the future.

By gaining more understanding and control over your feelings, you can start changing your behavior and have better relationships with others.

After gaining new skills on how to cope with your feelings, you can start creating some new positive habits. This step is fun, but it will also give you tools you can use to acquire many new positive habits in the future. We are habit creatures, and having some form of structure to our days can help us gain confidence and have extra energy for hobbies and creative projects.

Next, you can start building new relationships and improve the current ones. The most important relationship you will build is the relationship you have with yourself. When you love yourself and are sure of who you are, you can love others unconditionally and create stronger connections and better relationships. Because you are more authentic, you also attract people into your life that love you for who you are and notice your worth.

The final step is to rebuild your material world. This is less about acquiring new things and more about appreciating what you already have, understanding your personal style, what you want to have around you, and what makes you feel at peace.

If it sounds like a long journey and a lot of work, it's because it is. But I can assure you that you will be a completely new person when you finish all the steps. You will probably be more appreciative of what you have and feel more content with the little things in life, like being surrounded by people you love and enjoy spending time with, people who love you for who you are. It will be easier for you to know what you want and work towards your goals. And more importantly, you will know who you truly are.

In the last part of the book, I will share with you some practices that have helped me keep up the good work and live a happier life. These practices will help you maintain your well-being after facing change or difficult situations in your life. They will also help you keep the inner peace and happiness you have worked towards during the healing process.

Since change is the only constant thing in life, we cannot expect our lives to remain the same or have positive experiences all the time. However, when you have emotional stability, unshakable confidence, and inner peace, no occurrence in your external life will manage to bring you down again.

Before you start, I would like to remind you to be patient and compassionate with yourself as you take this journey to personal transformation because, depending on your situation and personality, completing the steps might take more or less time. My advice is to let go of all expectations and start the journey with an open mind.

How to Use This Book

You can use this book in different ways.

The first option is to read everything once to develop an idea of what you need to do and set a specific time to start the healing process, like a vacation or a less busy time.

This approach allows you to plan a specific time to do every step and to work on different steps simultaneously since you already know what will come next.

The second option is to start the healing process while you read the book. This approach is the better option if you prefer to focus on one thing at a time and truly complete every step before starting a new one.

I find this approach ideal because focusing on one thing allows you to enjoy the process and work at your own pace. It might also be a good option if you prefer to be excited about the next step without knowing what to expect.

Finally, you can use it as an inner work tool, an ongoing process. We never cease to heal and learn about ourselves, so the tools I will show you in the next chapters can stay with you for the rest of your life.

In my experience, healing is a layered process, and when we think we have completely released a specific situation, it might pop up again in the future for a deeper level of healing. So every time you feel something resurfacing, face a difficult situation, or simply feel stuck in life, not seeing the progress you expect, you can always return to this guideline and start the process again.

Regardless of how you approach and use this guide, the truth is that if you have the courage to take on this journey, you can gain a deeper self-understanding, heal from your past, and be well on your way to living a happier life.

Part 2: How to Let Go: A 5 Step Process

Thank you for embarking on this journey with me; you won't regret it. This part of the book will focus on the letting go process.

Letting go is very difficult for most of us because it means saying goodbye to parts of our past, parts of ourselves. It means that we are no longer the person we used to be, which can feel like a significant loss.

Letting go is also associated with resistance to change. Change can be uncomfortable because attachment to things, people, and ideas makes us feel safe and keeps us in our comfort zone. It takes a certain level of discomfort before a person decides to change. For example, because I feared change, it took me several years and increasingly bad experiences to realize that I couldn't continue working in a job that didn't fulfill me and where I wasn't appreciated.

Attachment is also difficult to release if you have low self-worth and self-esteem issues. You might believe you deserve the negative things, people, and situations in your life. You might also have the negative belief that you cannot be successful or achieve your goals. We continue accepting false friends, toxic partners, and even abuse because we think it is what we deserve due to our low self-esteem and self-worth. That is not true.

If you truly want to live a better life, it is very important to let go of everything that is not serving you anymore; you need to let go of everything that doesn't help you grow and instead holds you back. When you let go, you free yourself. You allow new and better things or people to come into your life and open yourself up to infinite possibilities.

Unfortunately, letting go is not always instant (although it can be); it is normally a process.

If you find it hard to let go, think of how you need to free up space and energy to do the things you want to do, focus on what you want to create, and spend time with people you love.

I wrote the sections in this book in a specific order to make it easier for you to detach and let go. Since the release process is not easy, starting with material things can help you get into the flow of letting go. It is also helpful to physically make room in your life to focus on deeper things instead of being distracted by clutter and stuff. That is why the first step is to let go of physical items.

Once you have more time and space in your physical life, you can start to value your relationships more and realize which of those relationships need work or are no longer healthy.

I will guide you step by step until you are happy with that area of your life. And remember that letting go doesn't always mean cutting contact with a person. It can also mean letting go of negative patterns in a relationship or learning how to set personal boundaries.

The third step will be to let go of bad habits. You will probably realize that cleaning up your space and reevaluating your relationships makes this part easier. It can be that you no longer spend time going out with people who were not truly there for you and with whom you used to drink a lot, which would make it easier to quit that habit. It can also be that you decide to set boundaries with a friend who takes advantage of your kindness, so it becomes easier to let go of your people-pleasing habit.

Getting rid of bad habits is also one of the steps that might take longer. I have different approaches that can help you, depending on your personality. We are all different. I have tried many different methods and techniques for reaching the same goal, and later in this guide, I will share several options that can make things easier for you.

Step four is about letting go of negative feelings, past trauma, and unresolved issues. It is about getting to know yourself better, understanding who you truly are, and finding out what you want to accomplish, not what society, friends, or family are imposing or suggesting you do. It doesn't matter how hard your life has been so far. You always have the power to heal yourself and let go.

This step is one of the most transformational ones. The more we hold on to trauma and emotions, the more we experience pain, disease, and illness. Emotions are energy that our bodies store. Thus, every negative emotion we don't process or release can potentially become a health issue in the future.

Our subconscious minds also store a memory screenshot of everything that happens in our lives, and even when we can't consciously remember a memory, it still impacts our thoughts and behaviors. But most importantly, having those unresolved issues doesn't allow you to be free. It is like a heavy weight you carry on your shoulders everywhere you go, one that weighs you down and makes it very hard for you to move forward. When you release everything from your past, you become light and ready to start something new.

With all the loss and inconsistency I suffered in my childhood, I had repressed many negative emotions stored in my body and subconscious mind. All these repressed feelings and unresolved issues surfaced simultaneously for resolution and release. That is why I think this step is so important to transform your life. I wish I had had the opportunity to plan when I wanted to deal with everything instead of having to do it when my life was already in complete chaos.

I have collected and explained some extremely powerful techniques that have the potency to help you deal with traumatic experiences and let go of repressed feelings. You can do it at your own pace and when you feel ready.

The last step of this part is to let go of your negative thoughts. By the time you get to this step, you will have used learned tools and strategies to gain more power over your life. Because of this, this step might be easier than you think.

When you let go of the negative self-talk, the irrational fears, the criticism, and the constant worry, you learn to love yourself better and see yourself in a different light. Everything around you becomes more positive and more enjoyable, and you start attracting better things in your life.

Step 1: Let Go of Material Possessions

"Don't hold on to material things for they can be replaced…Cherish and never let go of God, Family and Friends for they are irreplaceable"
-Carlos "Chuleto" Rodriguez

Welcome to your journey toward deep transformation.

The first step of this guideline is to let go of material things that no longer serve a purpose in your life and learn how to live with fewer material possessions.

Constant shopping and the nagging urge to own new material things like clothes, electronics, toys, and furniture reflect a state of uneasiness inside of us.

It might be that owning things makes you feel worthy or relevant. It can be that owning many things helps you boost your self-esteem or makes you feel like you belong to a certain group of people. Or it may be that you want to distract yourself from your feelings by investing time in shopping and purchasing things.

Constantly acquiring new things that we don't need can also be due to a need for instant gratification and dopamine release. Some people eat chocolate or sweets, others drink alcohol or take drugs, and others go shopping to feel good and receive a reward with new purchases.

No matter the reason, this step will help you let go of unnecessary things that no longer serve a purpose to make space for more important things: what truly makes you happy and has a real purpose in your present life. It will also help you reflect on your habits and relationships and the deep reasons why you own the things you own.

How to let go of material possessions

You are probably already familiar with the Konmari method and have perhaps even tried it. If you haven't heard about it, the Konmari method is a decluttering and organizing approach created by Japanese author Marie Kondo.

In her book, *"The Life-changing Magic Of Tidying Up,"* she explains a unique process we can use to start decluttering material possessions in our personal spaces, especially our homes.

Her method says you should declutter by category, not by area and that you should hold each item and try to gauge your body's reaction to it to identify if the item sparks joy or not. Fundamentally, the idea is to hold that piece of clothing, book, kitchen utensil, etc., and see if you feel happy around it.

She also proposes a specific category order where you start with easier things like clothes and move your way up to the most difficult ones, like sentimental items.

I highly recommend following the Konmari method to declutter the items in your house, office, or any personal space because it gives you a structured plan that makes it very easy to start and continue the decluttering process.

When you start with items like clothes, it gets easier to release other sentimental items once you realize that letting go feels like someone has lifted a weight off your shoulders.

However, you can also use any other decluttering method that works for you or declutter in any way you want. The important thing here is that you commit to making your personal spaces clutter free and surround yourself with things that have a purpose in your life.

These things can be useful things you use daily, like your favorite mug. They can be things that serve a specific purpose, like your special occasion shoes, or things that make you happy, like your book collection. Even decoration or other objects fulfill a purpose as long as they spark joy when you see them around.

Once you start decluttering, you will quickly realize that long-term joy comes from quality, not quantity. And this goes beyond the material quality and into how the item improves your quality of life. If you surround yourself with things that serve a purpose and make you happy and comfortable, you will not have the urge to buy more things all the time to try to fill a void. You will feel better in your personal space and be motivated to invest your time in doing things you consider very important.

That sounds exciting, right?

If you are ready to start decluttering, your first order of business is to commit to the process because the decluttering process can be overwhelming, depending on the amount of stuff you have. Committing to this process involves setting aside a specific time for the task and scheduling your cleaning and organizing time.

If you have a full-time job, schedule some time on the weekends, and don't worry about doing everything in the least amount of time possible; take your time to ensure you don't get overwhelmed.

Ask your friends and family to join you to make everything more fun. You can invite them to "clean and wine nights" and have fun in the process while you also donate some of the items you declutter. You can also organize garage sales and earn some money from all your extra possessions. Be creative and try to find a way to make it more enjoyable.

You can also start decluttering little by little. Start with one item daily and increase the number of items every day until you no longer find anything to declutter. Or you can do it all at once, perhaps by using your holidays for a complete home makeover.

Regardless of how you choose to do it, commit to completing the project, no matter how long it takes. It doesn't matter how long it takes. For me, decluttering has even become a lifestyle. I am very mindful of the new things I buy or bring into my life; and whenever I see something that doesn't serve me or that I don't like anymore, I sell it, donate it or get rid of it. That way, I don't start accumulating clutter again.

Once you have your schedule and have planned your decluttering days, you can look for inspiration to make starting easier. Thankfully, we have thousands of YouTube videos and other resources about decluttering and organizing that you can watch to gain motivation. You can also start a Pinterest board and save some home décor pictures of how you want your spaces to look once you have finished.

You can also set specific goals like, "I will only keep 15 pairs of shoes" or "My goal is to end up with five boxes in the garage." Having specific goals motivate you to start and keep going without giving up.

Once you start your decluttering process, you might find it very easy and exciting or extremely difficult. Don't be too hard on yourself when you begin struggling with letting things go —and you probably will when you start letting go of sentimental possessions. Instead, remind yourself that the essence of this process is to help you understand yourself and what you truly want better.

If you are used to accumulating things, you can ask yourself why that is the case and introspect to discover

43

the underlying reason why you feel secure by hanging on to material possessions.

I didn't have much growing up, so I would hold on to things out of fear of being unable to purchase more in the future. Perhaps you attach all your memories and emotions to your items or hold on to things for another reason. Whatever the case, try to dig deep and get to the root cause of your desire to hold on to things, even those that don't serve you.

Start with things that don't make you happy or those that make you feel bad when you look at them. Let go of the clothes that don't fit you and probably won't anymore or those that are so old that you can't wear nowadays. Release the things that you bought and have not used and make you feel guilt or regret. With time, you will realize you feel a lot better for not having those things.

If your main reason for not letting go of something that doesn't serve you is the idea of regretting getting rid of that thing in the future, let me tell you that you probably won't even remember you had it. If you keep what makes you happy, you won't miss things that were just there without a real purpose in your life.

It doesn't matter how you start. The important thing is what you learn in the process and how you feel when you complete decluttering. You will soon start noticing that you enjoy spending more time at home than before.

Growing up, I didn't enjoy being at home; I felt uncomfortable and preferred being outside. When I moved to my place, I realized that the main reason why I hated being at home was that it was always cluttered and disorganized. Because decluttering and tidying up have become a part of my life, I now enjoy being at home more than ever. I love the space I have created and only keep around the things that make me happy.

My decluttering journey started a few years ago after I had changed jobs and had a vacation period in between. It was around when my depression began, and it opened my eyes to the realization that I had built my life around my job. I didn't have any real hobbies then and had forgotten what I enjoyed and who I was. I had so many clothes in my wardrobe that I couldn't find anything to wear!

The year before I started my journey, I used to go shopping every weekend and would normally end up buying something to get instant gratification. I used shopping as a coping mechanism and a way to fill a void in my life. That vacation, I felt the urge to start cleaning up my apartment to feel better.

I dedicated my time to introspecting and figuring out what was happening and the kind of life I was building. Then, I stumbled upon some decluttering videos and decided to refresh my wardrobe to feel better about my clothes and to make it easier to find things to wear.

I soon realized that I had been hanging on to clothes I had owned for ten years or more. Some were in good condition, but I had not worn them in a very long time. I was amazed that I even brought all this stuff to Germany (that explains my two gigantic suitcases). In the past, when I wanted to declutter something, I would keep it "in case I needed it in the future." But I never needed it or wore it, and I can assure you that it rarely happens.

After getting rid of old clothes and shoes, I felt so good that day. It was easier to find things to wear, and my closet looked more polished and organized than ever.

Because my first decluttering process had been so therapeutic, I decided to reevaluate everything and declutter some more clothes that were not so old but that I didn't like. It took me a couple of months to let go of everything that I didn't need or didn't bring me joy, but the result was amazing.

The next step was to declutter all my other items: kitchen utensils, books, random things, paper, sentimental items, electronics, etc.

Before this, I had never considered myself someone who hangs on to things, but it can be very easy to attract clutter if you have enough space at home to store things. I cannot explain my relief after decluttering and clearing everything up. I loved how my apartment looked, and I felt lighter.

The process also brought me a better understanding of what I enjoyed. I remembered how much I love reading, and organizing my favorite books made me want to read them again. I also discovered my personal style and understood that I don't need a lot of clothes to feel trendy and look good. I can make so many outfits with my few clothing items that I never get bored. And I love all of them!

I also remembered what I loved to do as a kid. Besides reading and writing stories about my best friend and me, I also loved singing and dancing. As a child, I often spent the afternoon listening and singing along to Celine Dion's songs. My dad even bought me a karaoke microphone so I could sing as much as I wanted —our poor neighbors had to listen to me. This realization helped me start doing new things, like joining a salsa class to start dancing again.

Going through my personal things also made me think more about my past, especially when organizing my photos. I had been trying to forget my childhood and some of the trauma I had lived through by keeping myself very busy.

From the time I started college, I made sure I almost didn't have any free time in my week because I loved being busy. When I moved to Germany, I focused on working hard because it made me feel good, and I could avoid dealing with all my unresolved feelings.

Looking at my childhood photos brought up many memories, some of which were beautiful, like the song my sister and I used to dance to all the time in the garden when we came home from school or when my brother and I were very young, and watched his favorite movie Hercules cuddling in the sofa (we watched it so many times that I knew all the lines).

But I also remembered how my aunt and cousins passed away while still young and how I had struggled with an eating disorder for so long. Because this was the first time I thought about all those things, it made me feel deep pain.

So, be ready to unravel some things about yourself during this process. This is part of the plan, and I assure you that you will have managed to deal with all those emotions by steps 4 and 5.

Don't try to ignore your feelings or the things that come up. Instead, give yourself permission to grieve, be angry, and feel your guilt or pain. That is the first step towards letting go.

Step 2: Re-evaluate Relationships

I encourage you to complete step one before starting the next step.

However, if you have already started and are making good progress, you can go ahead and work on step two at the same time. But let me warn you: this step might open up some wounds. Be ready to open yourself up to feeling pain and sadness but also joy and relief.

Step two is about evaluating the people in your life to ensure that everyone around you is a positive influence on you. You have probably heard thousands of times that you should stay away from toxic people and be careful of the company you keep. However, if you are anything like me, you have probably not done anything substantial to ensure that you only keep the company of people who positively impact you.

You probably agree that you have in your life some people who are hurtful or who damage your life, but because you are also afraid of what the other person would think, you find it very hard to detach yourself from them. Don't worry; you shouldn't be hard on yourself during this process.

It is not easy to cut off relationships, even if they are toxic to us or when people show us that they are not our true friends or don't want our best interests. While that may be the case, it is important to remember that you "are" the people you surround yourself with.

If you spend your time with negative, frustrated, and angry people who only try to put you down and steal your energy, you will soon start thinking this behavior is normal or even start acting like them. Therefore, this step is important if you want to transform your life.

Let's first define a toxic relationship.

What is a toxic relationship?

For me, a toxic relationship is a relationship that doesn't contribute anything to my physical, mental, or emotional well-being and is, instead, harmful to my physical, mental, or emotional integrity and self-esteem. It is a relationship that is damaging for one or both parties.

There can be several degrees of toxicity in a relationship. From negativity, passive-aggressiveness and manipulation to physical, psychological and emotional abuse. It can go from a person that puts you down to make themselves feel better to someone who is physically and mentally abusive.

No matter in which part of the spectrum, a toxic negative relationship makes you feel defensive, uneasy and unsafe. It doesn't bring the best in you and doesn't contribute to your happiness and wellbeing.

Some of these relationships might be evident to you. For example, if you have a classmate that bullies you, it is evident that it is a toxic relationship and should want this person out of your life. However, these relationships can also be very subtle, and you might not realize it until you start this step. It can be a friend who uses passive-aggressive comments to make you feel guilty or insecure. Or a family member who guilt trips you to make you do what they want.

How to reevaluate your relationships

To understand how your relationships work, start by creating a list of all the people around you. Rank them from the ones you have more contact with to the ones you have the least contact with, and add the percentage of time you spend a week with the person. The five people you spend more time with are the ones who influence your life the most, from how you think to the way you talk and the words you use.

I spend most of my time with my husband, and it is funny how we have reached a level of synergy that we have started using the same vocabulary and speaking mannerisms. I noticed that when I started using a new word, it was usually because he had used it a lot, and I had picked it up from him. That also happens to me with accents.

I remember when I was young, I spent a lot of time with a friend from the north of Mexico and soon started to speak with his accent melodiously even though I hadn't been to his city before.

These are only silly examples of how the people around you greatly influence you. You can easily adapt to the values, thought patterns, and behavior of the people around you. Even if you don't, you can start seeing it as normal.

Since I have worked in different companies, I could easily identify the different corporate cultures that each of them had. And it was fascinating to see how, after a few months, new colleagues would start acting, talking, and behaving like the people working there. I found that dynamic to be true both in positive and uplifting environments, as well as in more negative fear-based ones.

After creating your list of regular contacts and the amount of time you spend with them, start thinking about your relationship with each person. Notice how you feel when you think about them, and try to describe your relationship in 5 to 10 words. Be very honest.

Reflect on how you feel when you are with the person, what you normally do, how you feel after spending time with them, and if you feel excited to see them or if it feels like a burden. Think about why you feel that way and write everything next to your list. This part is not about judging the other person; it is about understanding the pattern and the type of people in your circle.

Take the time to evaluate your relationships and, most importantly, be honest about your thoughts and feelings. It is not about judging or trying to rationalize it. Write everything as it comes to you first. You will probably notice a pattern or realize that you surround yourself with the same type of people. You might even realize that you spend most of your time with people you don't choose to spend time with. No matter what you discover, it is important to get back to your list after a few days or one week and see if what you wrote the first day still feels right.

When I started this process, what helped me the most was looking for patterns in people around me and past relationships. I looked back to my friends since I was very young, my romantic relationships, and my family. This process made me realize the type of people I was attracting into my life and in which situations.

So, after you are happy with your list of current relationships, start thinking about your past friendships, dates, and other types of relationships and try to identify the patterns.

I immediately noticed that some of my romantic relationships before I met my husband were very damaging. Some of my high school or college dates were manipulative, made me feel bad about myself, and didn't really care about me. One of them was also psychologically abusive to the point that it took me a long time to recover from the damage he caused.

When I wondered why my husband was different and how I managed to break the pattern with him, I realized that I met abusive men during moments of insecurity when I didn't feel good enough. How could I find guys to respect me if I didn't respect myself? It seemed like I attracted the exact kind of relationship I didn't want.

And the funny thing is that I met many loving and caring people as well, but I didn't find them attractive at the time. When I met my husband, I had already learned that lesson. That's why I attracted something different.

I also identified the kind of friends I had through the years. This is an area I have always felt very good about, especially in my younger years.

I believe that friends are the family you choose. I can honestly say that all the friends I kept in my life are beautiful, loving, and caring people; and even if I lost touch with some of them, I feel so lucky to have had them in my life.

But a few years before my depression started, I had also been attracting other types of friends. One day, my husband and I realized that a group of friends we had built was not supportive or encouraging, but quite the opposite.

We would travel hours to visit them only to return home feeling down and with the need to talk for hours about what had happened. They were always complaining about everything and always feeling like victims of what happened to them, even though it was evident to us that most of their problems were the consequences of their actions.

They would ignore me when I was speaking, use passive-aggressive comments to make me and my husband feel bad, and never voiced any meaningful support for our plans and ideas. It was not a pleasant time, but I was amazed at how long we kept those friends.

Think about all the types of relationships you have built. See if you attract specific types of people in certain periods of your life and think about how you felt when you met the people you love spending time with. After engaging in this exercise, you will have a more profound understanding of your relationships and probably identify the ones that are not contributing to your growth and happiness.

Let me note that having a friend who complains to you about having a rough time or a specific problem does not mean the relationship is toxic. We all go through difficult periods in life and might not always have a positive mindset, which is ok.

What you want to identify is if it is a pattern that has lasted a long time and if the person tries to bring you down.

Even when I was depressed and wasn't positive, I never tried to harm the people around me. A good friend who loves you will always want the best for you, even if he/she is going through a difficult time.

Let me also highlight that if you are in a physically or emotionally abusive relationship with a partner or another person, seek help as quickly as possible. I know it might be extremely hard, or you may think you will feel lost without the person, but please, take it seriously because such a relationship can have deeply negative consequences. A violent person will not stop without professional help.

Violence and aggression normally start with being angry and losing the temper from time to time or emotionally manipulating, but both can quickly turn into physical aggression. Violence also increases over time. If your partner raises a hand on you once, he/she will probably do it again and then do it more often.

Intrafamilial violence is a real issue in the world. Even developed countries have astounding rates of intrafamilial violence, especially towards women. I know it can be very easy to believe that an abusive person can change, but you cannot help them.

A person who reaches those levels of violence normally has deep-rooted pain, and only professional help and self-awareness can change them. So please, if you are in a violent relationship, look for help immediately. Additionally, you can reach out to organizations that can help you escape abusive relationships and build a better future, even if you have kids.

Let's go back to the list!

By now, you should have a good overview of the type of people you have in your life and how your relationships are. It is time to act and start improving your relationships.

Start with the people you spend most of your time with, like your partner, family members, coworkers, classmates, etc., and go through the list until you finish with the last person. Write the answers to the questions below so you can reflect on them and decide what steps to take.

1. Select the people you love spending time with. The ones who uplift you, care about you and love you for who you are.

2. Identify the ones that don't bring anything positive to your life and normally make you feel bad about yourself.

3. Note if this has been a pattern or something caused by a specific situation in the person's life.

4. Define if you have chosen to have them in your life and if you would like to keep the relationship. In some cases, completely separating from a person is not possible, but you can choose to limit your contact and set boundaries.

5. List the things you would like to change or improve about the relationship. Include what you could change and what the other person can change on their part.

6. If it is a damaging or toxic relationship, think about the behaviors or patterns both you and the other person have that contributed to the situation.

After going through the list, select the relationships you feel good with and the people who make you happy and are a support system in your life. These are your most important social circle. Take a minute to appreciate them and thank them for being in your life. Now, focus on the relationships that need improvement.

How to improve your relational synergy

The first step is to identify what has gone wrong in the relationship and what all involved can do better. It is very important to take responsibility for our behaviors and actions that might have affected the relationship and design a plan to change them.

For example, if you find that your relationship with your partner has become distant, think about what you did to contribute to it. Maybe you stopped showing affection and interest, and the other person felt rejected.

Or perhaps you feel you have been taken advantage of by a friend, but it was because you could never say no. Think about the boundaries you need to set to make the relationship healthier for you. Before discarding a relationship, consider what you and the other party can do to improve it.

In most cases, it is nobody's fault. We often find ourselves in negative relationships because there is something to be learned. And both parties have specific traits that make the relationship difficult. So, there is no need to blame anyone.

However, this does not apply to abusive relationships. I cannot stress enough how important it is to walk away from any relationship with people that are mentally, emotionally, or physically abusive toward you.

If you realize that a person has always behaved the same and there is a pattern, or if you think the person doesn't want to change, I would also seriously consider removing them from my life or setting firm boundaries with them. That is what I did with a friend that was passive-aggressive toward me.

I realized that she used those passive-aggressive comments and subtle insults when she felt bad about herself.

She wanted to project all her negative feelings onto me and use me to make herself feel better. When I realized that I was the one allowing the behavior by not setting boundaries and spending time with her, regardless of how mean she was to me, I decided to end the friendship. I felt there was no point in continuing the relationship with that person, and I started valuing myself more after making that decision.

Evaluating people in your life can be specially challenging when it comes to family members. If you have tried many times to improve the relationship, but it hasn't worked, the chances are high that this relationship is not healthy for you.

Sometimes we feel guilty because we have grown up learning that family is the most important thing in life. However, although I also consider family very important, I believe that setting strong boundaries with family members that don't appreciate us or show us respect is an act of self-love. We can love them from a distance without letting them affect our life.

It is important to identify which relationships are worth keeping, how to improve them, and which ones are no longer in the highest good of all involved. I believe people deserve second chances, and unless it concerns an abusive relationship, healthy boundaries and a good conversation with the person can help you improve the relationship. If there is no improvement or the person doesn't show any interest in having a conversation and making things better, separation from that person might be a better approach.

After some negative experiences, I learnt how to deal with people who don't respect others and with whom it's impossible to have direct, honest communication. I usually tried several times to speak directly to the person to solve the problem, but it would only worsen everything.

If you have tried several times to have a conversation with the person and it didn't work: Develop a strategy not to let the things the person says affect you and set healthy boundaries.

How to set boundaries

I have continuously repeated myself during this section talking about setting healthy boundaries. But what do I really mean by that?

The official definition of boundary is to set a limit, or a line that marks a limit to an area. What I mean by setting boundaries with other people is to define the lines that we are not ok with them crossing. It is to respect our needs and make sure that they are met. And to put a stop to situations that make us feel uncomfortable.

Setting a boundary can be absolutely anything, it all depends on the situation and person you are dealing with. From saying no to a friend when you feel tired to go out, to stop spending time with people that don't value and appreciate you. It can be as simple as not answering the phone when you don't feel like talking or asking a person not to visit you without previous notice. And it can go as far as removing yourself from a situation you are not comfortable with, like walking away from someone who disrespects you.

The same way we set boundaries with kids, who are still learning how to navigate this experience, we need to do it with other adults, especially if they don't respect our needs. This is a big lesson I had to learn in my adult years.

Since I was young, I got used to please others to avoid having negative consequences. I tried to always be nice, specially to my parents, to avoid the punishment that would come as a consequence of not doing what they wanted me to. I grew up so scared of upsetting someone else, that I allowed all types of behaviors toward me, even to my detriment.

After all the negative experiences I went through for not setting boundaries, I finally understood that I needed to honor my needs as well. It started when I walked away from a workplace where I was not respected, and continued by doing small things like saying no when something made me feel uncomfortable.

Little by little, I chose myself and listened to my needs, instead of doing what other people wanted me to do. And, like everything we repeatedly do, it became a habit. It is now natural to me to respect my limits and honestly communicate when something is not ok for me.

Sometimes we feel that setting a boundary can upset or make the other person feel bad. In my experience, that is not the case. I have realized that healthy adults don't mind when we say no or set a limit, and actually respect it. When we communicate our needs in an honest and respectful way, the other person will likely be glad to make us feel good and comfortable.

People who don't respect your boundaries or are upset that you set them, might feel entitled to take something from you. It can be energy, money, time or emotional support. Whatever it might be, you are never obliged to do things you are not comfortable with. In those cases, even stronger boundaries are needed with that person or situation.

The key to healthy happy relationships is to make sure everyone feels content with what it is asked from them;

that is, when everyone's needs are considered. For example: there are people who need their space and want to be by themselves from time to time. That doesn't mean they don't cherish their relationships; it just means that they have a boundary in that regard.

When we put ourselves in other people's shoes, it is easier for us to accept and respect their boundaries and understand where they come from. And it becomes easier to set our own as well.

Since other people in our lives are important, this process might release feelings of not being good enough, abandonment issues, and other deep emotions. That is because it is not easy to evaluate people in our lives, especially if we have created a strong bond with them or are in a codependent relationship. Separating from some people, even those abusive towards us can feel like a great loss.

Going through a loss is difficult and emotional; therefore, let yourself grieve and feel sad about losing a friend, family member, or partner. Forgive the person for the pain he/she caused you, and move on when you feel ready. I like a technique called **Ho'oponopono** to help release the pain or grief associated with a relationship. I explain the technique in detail in the next chapter, but it is mainly about forgiveness.

Forgiveness

The next step involves forgiving yourself and others for everything that happened in the past.

By forgiving yourself, you let go of the feelings of guilt and shame and become more empowered. You learn from your mistakes but don't let them haunt you and bring you down.

By forgiving others, you cut the invisible cord that connects you with this other person and releases it. Even if the person did a horrible unjustifiable thing to you, forgiving gives you freedom and helps you regain your power.

If you find it difficult to forgive someone, be compassionate and see the other person from another perspective. See the pain they have gone through that has made them behave that way. We normally do the best we can with the tools and state of consciousness we have at the moment.

Forgiveness does not mean the action was ok or that you should allow the person back into your life. It is a gift we give ourselves to stop carrying the burden and set ourselves free from that person or situation.

Forgiving ourselves is also important.

For example, I carried a weighty load of guilt for allowing myself to stay in abusive relationships and for not saying anything afterward. I can honestly say that it took me a long time to forgive myself and release those emotions.

I was also carrying a lot of guilt for harming myself during my eating disorder period. It has taken me several years to release the guilt completely and truly forgive myself. However, as I penned down my story in the first part, some remains started pouring out. I started feeling very emotional and took some time off to understand what was happening until I realized that I still felt guilty about my eating disorder.

If you are also struggling with this step, remember that you are HUMAN and start thinking of yourself as such. We all go through difficult experiences and sometimes develop coping mechanisms that are detrimental to us but be sure that you did everything you could with what you had at the moment, and THAT IS OK. Think that what happened left you with a valuable lesson that you can use now to improve your life. You also decided to change, which is a big step towards self-love and personal growth. And you have the rest of your life to learn from it and do it differently.

Forgiving others and ourselves is not easy and might take some time, but at the end of this process, you will start valuing yourself and your relationships more. You will identify what you can improve to ensure you don't end up in toxic relationships again and start healing so you can attract people who are better for you into your life.

Even if you feel grief for letting someone go, think about the emotional health benefits of not being around a person who doesn't appreciate you. You are a beautiful human being who deserves love and respect. If you start healing yourself, loving yourself, and valuing yourself, you will soon surround yourself with people who share your values, want the best for you, and love you for who you are.

Step 3: Get Rid Of Toxic Habits

If you have reached this third step, you might still be grieving the loss of the people who are no longer in your life, and you are probably dealing with many emotions and feelings, from anger to grief. This is all normal and part of the process, so remember not to be hard on yourself.

Because we are all connected, we create an attachment with people in our lives, even if they have a damaging effect on us. Although this can be a very difficult time, allow yourself to feel and process the feelings, and do not try to escape them with bad habits that will only damage you in the long run.

If you feel that releasing emotions and pain associated with what happened to others is too overwhelming, you can also go to step 4 first and come back to this chapter afterward.

This step is all about getting rid of the negative habits we have accumulated in our lives. You have already started this process by solving your problems with the people around you. Identifying your own negative patterns in relationships and taking responsibility for them, empowers you to change them.

You need the same attitude when trying to eliminate other unhealthy habits like smoking, drinking, binge eating, gambling, eating disorders, shopping, etc.

Essentially, you need the same attitude towards any behaviors that may compromise your physical, mental, or emotional health or keep you from reaching your highest potential and living a fulfilled life.

Now let me just clarify that not because I label something as "bad habit" means that it is bad for you. It is not about being judgmental of the things we do and how we behave, but to know that we can improve everything that is not in alignment with our health and well-being.

We all have habits and patterns that act as coping mechanisms and we have adopted as ways to relieve pain or avoid it, and it is completely normal to have them. However, if we want to improve our lives, we need to be willing to let some of them go, specially if they are causing us imbalances in life.

This step will also not be easy because, as you shall see in step 9, creating a habit requires repeating the action or behavior many times. Habits work in a loop: there is always a trigger or cue, then the routine, and finally, a reward. The reward refers to the chemicals released in our brain, like Dopamine, Serotonin, and other feel-good hormones.

The habit loop is stored in your subconscious mind, and you start the routine every time the cue or pattern appears because your brain knows there will be a reward afterward. Sometimes it can feel like we have lost control and let the habit take over our lives, which is what happened to me with my eating disorder.

But even though getting rid of habits might not feel like an easy task, it is only a matter of having the right mindset and motivation to change.

A realistic, how-to approach to habit change

First, you need to take responsibility for your actions. This step is important because it ensures you don't feel like a victim stuck in a situation out of your control. It is important to remember that you still have the mind that decided to start a habit; that means you also have the power to stop doing it or replace it with a healthy one.

As you have probably heard, the first step towards habit change is accepting your situation and realizing the behavior has become damaging for you.

This doesn't mean that you should blame yourself or feel guilt about it. We all have negative patterns and behaviors, it is part of the human experience!

In fact, I invite you to be compassionate with yourself and even with the habit because it helped you in some way or another, else you wouldn't even have it.

I suffered from eating disorders for a long time during my adolescence. When I was 13, I moved to another city and to a new school. Before that, I had lived in a small city where I knew most of the people my age and had a group of friends who loved me and accepted me for who I was. Because I had never experienced such a change before, I became very self-conscious. I was also taking on a lot of responsibilities at home because my mom worked a lot, and we didn't have help from others, so it became very overwhelming to be in the process of puberty and also taking care of my siblings.

One day, I read a book about a girl who had bulimia. The book's target audience was adolescents, and its purpose was to create eating disorders awareness and help this age group understand how damaging they could be. I didn't learn much from the book, but it gave me some ideas on how I could start losing weight. I remember feeling very guilty when eating junk food or sweets until, one day, it seemed easier to just throw it up.

I started feeling very guilty about restricting my food or throwing up, so there were periods when I tried to eat healthily and stay away from those habits, but it wouldn't last. Whenever I had a stressful situation, I would binge eat and then throw up again. Or just restrict my calories so much that I was barely eating. It became a harrowing cycle because I carried a lot of guilt for treating my body like that, but I felt I couldn't stop.

One day after 8 or 9 years of suffering from Bulimia on and off, I hit rock bottom and decided that I didn't want to do this again. Ever. I accepted I had a problem and needed to change. I then immediately decided never to put myself in that situation ever again. It was a really hard process, and more than once, I was tempted to throw up the food I had eaten. But I used exercise as a new habit that allowed me to overwrite the eating disorder with a healthier, better habit.

Exercise helped me process all the underlying emotions causing my eating disorder; it helped me feel better about myself and gain more confidence. So I exchanged the old pattern of behavior for a new one. I also started working on healing my root problem, which was that I didn't feel good enough and didn't feel loved.

I choose to tell you my story to let you know that if I could change the behavior after so many years, you can too. My eating disorder could have killed me, but I managed not to let it by finding the motivation to get out of there.

You can do the same too. It doesn't matter if your habits are more or less damaging than mine; it is possible to change everything if we want to and put effort towards it.

You can overcome every negative habit and replace it with something healthier.

The first step is to accept that you have a problem or a habit that no longer serves you and then gauge your willingness to change it. A good motivator can also be the key to releasing negative habits or patterns of behavior.

Since we are all different and struggling with different negative habits or patterns, no rule fits all situations. Instead, I will share with you four tools or methods I used in different scenarios to change my habits, patterns, or addictions.

1: Replace it with a new one

My first strategy, and one of the most successful ones I've ever used, is to change your habit by creating a new one. We normally hear that it takes 21 days to create a habit, but in my opinion, it can also take longer, depending on what it is.

So your commitment to the new habit is key to getting rid of the old one. In step 6 of the book, I will discuss creating healthy habits, but you can start by finding something you can trade for your negative pattern.

When I was working to overcome my eating disorder, I started exercising or going for a walk whenever I felt the need to binge eat. I traded the binge eating habit for something healthier that had a similar effect at the moment: helping me deal with stress and emotional pain. If I couldn't go for a run or a walk, I would drink a cup of tea, which also helped me relax and feel better.

If you use this approach to replace one habit with another, remember that the cue or trigger should be the same to ensure your brain is programmed to stop the old routine and start the new one every time the trigger or cue appears. The trigger can be anything: a place, an action, a smell, or an emotion. When the brain identifies the trigger, the routine will start because the brain is waiting for the reward afterward. When we change the routine using the same trigger, it erases the old behavior from our memory.

When I struggled with Bulimia, my triggers were deep emotions and stressful situations. If I had a stressful situation at home or school, I would binge eat, then throw everything up. To change the pattern, I chose to exercise instead. I would go for a run or a spinning class to release the negative emotions; the rewards were the endorphins that my brain produced afterward.

At first, it took a lot of determination and discipline to choose exercise over eating and to fight with my brain so I would follow the habit loop I had created. And to be honest with you, I failed more than one time. But with time, it became a new habit, and I didn't even think about food when I felt bad; I just wanted to get some fresh air or put in a run.

This also works with negative behavior patterns. When I had social anxiety and negative thought patterns, I would start worrying about what others thought of me and what they thought of my anxiety symptoms until it became a full-blown anxiety attack. After some years of dealing with anxiety, I began changing the negative pattern by practicing mindfulness. When anxiety kicked in, I would then focus on objects, smells, and colors in the room to redirect my focus to something else. With time, it became easier and easier to stop anxiety attacks, and I started feeling more relaxed around other people.

2: The cold turkey approach

Another way to approach habit change is to go cold turkey and just stop. This approach requires you to be very disciplined and strong-minded but can be very beneficial.

My mom smoked for around 30 years of her life. She started very young, during her teens (she grew up in the '70s), and became addicted to nicotine and relied on cigarettes to release stress. She stopped smoking during her pregnancies but soon got back into the habit. After she and my dad divorced, she decided to quit smoking because she wanted to transform her life. One day during our vacation, she just stopped buying cigarettes. She changed her look, renewed her wardrobe, and stopped smoking. She has gone more than 20 years without touching a cigarette again, no matter how much stress or anxiety she has felt.

This approach requires a lot of determination, no one can dispute that, but the most important thing to quit a habit cold turkey is to have the right motivation and desire to change.

My mom truly wanted to transform her life and knew that smoking was not good for her health, which made her determined to make a change. What helped her stay focused was her motivation. Because she was now separated from my dad and lived as a single mom, she felt responsible for being there for my siblings and me and understood that her health was extremely important.

You can also use this approach to deal with procrastination. If it is tough to do what you need to do or work on your goals and you want to stop the pattern, I recommend you read the book *5-Second-Rule* by Mel Robbins.

In her book, Mel explains how you can stop procrastination and change your actions by stopping your automatic behavior and engaging your prefrontal cortex. The prefrontal cortex is the part of your brain engaged when making conscious decisions; you can activate it by counting backward from 5 to 1. After activating this part, you are likelier to make a conscious decision and stop the autopilot behavior or habit.

Mel stumbled onto the rule one day when she decided to get out of bed without hitting the snooze button by thinking she was a rocket about to be launched and counted 5...4...3...2...1. This five-second rule is extremely helpful for breaking procrastination patterns and overcoming most of your unhealthy habits.

You can still benefit from this tool even if you don't have such damaging behaviors or addictions.

Consider an example where you struggle with motivation to exercise, have a sugar addiction, or would like to stop spending so much time on social media or watching Netflix. You can use the 5- second rule to avoid making excuses on why you shouldn't go to the gym or get out off your couch and act.

However, as powerful as this tool can be, the first step to using it is accepting your situation and truly committing to change. If you desire it and put your effort into it, there is nothing you cannot achieve.

3: Make tiny/little changes

The third option I can recommend you use to release a negative habit is to make little changes instead of drastic ones. You can use this approach when you could have side effects from withdrawal, in case of substance abuse, or your habit is not so damaging, and you don't want to get rid of it completely, like watching too much TV or spending too much time on social media.

In such cases, I would advise you to create a plan that outlines a gradual approach to changing your actions and eventually reaching a comfortable point. You can start setting some boundaries, like only scrolling on social media for a specific amount of time a day, and gradually reduce it until you reach your goal. Or you could start reducing your sugar consumption gradually until you are happy with your daily consumption.

This could also work with binge shopping. Not many people talk about it, but binge shopping is a serious addiction that gives us instant gratification and increased dopamine levels. For many people, it is an escape from problems and a way to feel better about themselves, if only for a little while. Since it is not realistic to stop shopping —after all, we need to buy some things— the best way to overcome binge shopping is to set gradual goals to reach a point where it is no longer a bad habit. Setting rules like how often you go shopping, writing a shopping list, and defining a weekly budget can help you regain control over your shopping habits.

If you have already completed working through step 1 of this book, you may have realized that you have a shopping addiction and have already decided to be more mindful about the things you bring into your life. Nevertheless, a defined strategy can help you control your spending habits and eliminate binge shopping.

4: Seek professional help

Before you get mad at me for talking about binge shopping, I just want to clarify that there is nothing wrong with shopping or wanting to purchase new things. It becomes detrimental when it is done without being mindful about it and causes financial and/or emotional distress. Or when it is just a mechanism to avoid our feelings and emotions. But if your job revolves around it or your social life benefits from it, I wouldn't consider it a negative habit.

The last strategy would be to seek professional help.

If none of the three above strategies have worked for you or your plan hasn't been successful, and you find yourself trapped in the same negative pattern again, you can always seek help.

You can seek help from family members or friends you can call or send a message to whenever you feel the need to do something you don't want to. Or it can be looking for professional help like a counselor, therapist, hypnosis expert, or support group. No matter which option appeals to you, the key thing to remember is that it is ok to seek help, and you have many resources available to you if you truly want to change your life.

No matter what your bad habit is and how much you are willing to change it, to obtain permanent results, it helps to focus on solving the root issue of the problem.

Most of our negative patterns and addictions come from the same place: unsolved trauma, stress, feelings of unworthiness, feeling that we are not enough, and lack of loving and meaningful relationships. It is amazing to start getting rid of bad habits, but until we solve the core issue, we will still struggle to get into the same pattern or another damaging one. This is the most difficult and most important part of the healing process.

In the next chapter, I will help you identify your unresolved issues and share some tools you can use to release them.

We all carry deep-rooted childhood traumas that define our behavior patterns and belief system. By releasing some of the negative emotions associated with them, we free ourselves from our past and free up some space to move forward.

At this point, you have probably managed to take away distractors in your life, from useless things to negative relationships and unhealthy habits, which has opened up some time and space to focus on your emotional state.

When we are calm without so many distractions, unresolved issues and unprocessed emotions start resurfacing. Do not be hard on yourself during this process, and don't fight it.

The techniques I shall share in the next step have helped me heal all the wounds I have mentioned at various points in this book and some other unprocessed trauma. They allowed me to transform into a better version of myself.

Step 4: Release Negative Emotions

For most people, this is the hardest step of them all. We are not used to confronting our insecurities, past traumas, and unresolved feelings. We are designed to create defense mechanisms that help us forget, ignore, or repress emotions and memories that cause us pain.

As Dr. David Hawkins explains in his book *Letting Go*, we either repress, suppress, or express the negative emotions we experience. Unfortunately, none of those mechanisms helps us release emotions.

Our bodies and minds have an innate desire to avoid pain at all costs. Still, we store the pain we suffered in past experiences in our emotional body and subconscious mind, which keeps us from moving forward and developing better habits.

Many of our behavioral traits relate to the defense mechanisms we have built during our lifetime to cope with pain and stress or to avoid reliving it. If we were victims of bullying at school, we might have developed some insecurities that we try very hard to cover to avoid another experience like the one we had growing up. It can be that we don't let people in or create a façade to cover up our true personalities.

The same can happen if someone we have trusted and loved, like a parent, teacher, or close friend, betrays us. We develop behavioral patterns to protect ourselves from re-suffering the pain we felt in the past, but that doesn't allow us to reach our potential.

We carry those unresolved feelings and emotions like a heavy burden, even though they are detrimental to our emotional well-being and physical health. Since our emotions are energy, we store them in our emotional bodies as negative energy. With time, the stored negative energy affects the cells in our bodies and can even cause disease and illness.

In addition to the negative emotion, we can create an associated belief that triggers us to have a specific behavioral pattern. For example, if we felt rejected by our parents when we were children, we might believe that we don't deserve to feel heard or that we are not worthy. Due to that belief, we might allow people to cross our boundaries because we think we don't deserve to have needs, that we deserve abusive behavior, or that what we have to say is not important.

To change the limiting belief and create a new pattern, we need to release the emotion associated with it. When we release the emotion from our bodies, the thoughts also stop having importance, and we can easily change our beliefs and create new behavioral patterns.

But how do we start releasing all these negative emotions? How do we face these past traumas? How do we even recognize which events in our lives were so traumatic to us that they changed our behaviors?

Believe me when I say that this is not an easy task.

Sometimes we have buried these memories so deeply in our subconscious that we don't even remember them. And sometimes, these events are too painful to remember, and we are too scared to open those pandora boxes, which is why we prefer to avoid facing them by distracting ourselves with something else.

While it is not easy to heal from our past, it is worth it because when we release negative emotions, we feel lighter, happier, more motivated, and more emotionally stable. We can get rid of the patterns that keep us from achieving our highest potential and start building the life we want.

Before I start describing some methods you can use to release these emotions and traumas, I would like to write a disclaimer for everyone who has lived through extremely traumatic events like childhood abuse, rape, kidnapping, and violent attacks, among others.

Although these exercises can be very helpful for pain release, relieving the memories can be retraumatizing. Therefore, I highly recommend seeking help from a professional therapist who can help you apply these methods if you think they could be detrimental to you. You can also ask a close friend or family member to support you during the process. Only when you feel ready to face your unsolved feelings and past traumas should you practice these techniques by yourself.

Through my healing process, I have tried the techniques I explain below and found them useful for different types of healing. Since we are all different, try the ones that resonate with you, and don't be scared to mix and match these exercises to achieve your goals. When practicing them, your inner, all-knowing self will tell you what to do and what feels right for you.

Experience and release the emotion

When facing the negative emotions I became conscious of, I would use Dr. David Hawkins's Letting Go technique to release them. He suggests letting the emotion "be" without trying to suppress it, repress it, or express it. Just sit with the emotion, and be aware of the pain, discomfort, or how it feels in the body. Surrender control and the need to change it. The less we resist the emotion, the faster we will let it go. This approach is especially useful when feelings of guilt or shame come to the surface.

When we make a mistake or have some regret, it is common to experience guilt or shame. Although it can be painful and uncomfortable to have these feelings, the best way to release them is to let them be, feel them in our bodies, and forgive ourselves for whatever happened. I consider this technique a very quick and easy way to let those negative emotions go, and it works with any negative emotion we experience.

When we experience an emotion and receive the message the emotion wants to give us, it fulfills the emotion's purpose, rendering its existence unnecessary. It also helps us see things from a different perspective, forgive ourselves and others and learn the lesson we need to learn from that experience.

This technique has been especially helpful for me in releasing the feelings of shame and guilt I felt after being bullied and slandered at work. I was publicly shamed in a horrible way, which left me feeling unworthy, and as if I were faulty and deserved the abuse. I also felt guilty and angry at myself for not doing anything to defend myself. I felt I had given up on myself.

It took a long time to let those feelings go and to release the pain from that experience, but when I was ready, I decided to face the pain and let the emotions flow without resistance. I felt the shame like a storm running through my body. And the guilt was like a knife in my stomach. It was a very painful moment, but I just let it happen and focused on my breath until the emotions were no longer there.

When I felt better, I decided to forgive myself for what had happened and forgive the people involved, thinking we all did the best we could with what we had.

After releasing the emotions, I understood that people who can be so cruel to others are people who have also suffered from abuse or pain. Although it doesn't justify what they did because we can all choose to be better, it helped me have compassion for others and made it easier to forgive.

This process of letting go is very quick. Fortunately, when we stop fighting the emotion, let it tell us what we need to hear, and then acknowledge it without resistance, we release it immediately.

EFT Tapping

The Emotional Freedom Technique, or EFT Tapping, is one of the most powerful tools I have tried so far to release negative emotions, solve past traumas, overcome depression and anxiety, and even get rid of bad habits or addictive patterns.

This technique is based on traditional Chinese medicine, where meridian points are thought of as areas of the body energy flows through. These pathways help balance the energy flow to maintain your body healthy, and any imbalance can influence disease or sickness.

When our emotional body stores negative energy or has energy blockages due to a traumatic experience, the energy flow of the entire body gets disrupted, and disease or sickness might appear.

EFT Tapping focuses on releasing the energy blockages to restore a healthy energy flow in our bodies. By restoring this energy balance, the symptoms a negative experience or emotion may have caused might also get relieved.

Like Acupuncture, EFT uses meridian points of energy, but instead of applying pressure with needles, it uses fingertip tapping, hence the name. Tapping these energy hot spots helps you access your body's energy and send signals to your subconscious mind and to the part of the brain that controls stress levels. Therefore, tapping can reduce the stress or the negative emotion you feel from a traumatic event and restore the balance in your energy flow.

EFT tapping usually involves five main steps. The sequence is repeatable until the issue or negative emotion disappears. That means it might take a couple of tapping rounds, some weeks, or even months of regular practice, depending on the situation and how deeply it affected you.

1. The first step is to identify the issue, negative emotion, or traumatic situation you want to heal from. Through the tapping rounds, the issue will be the focal point. This allows you to feel the emotions associated with the situation and command your brain to de-stress, which helps you release the energy blockage.

2. The second step is to test the initial intensity of the feeling involved. After you identify the issue or situation, you need to set a level of the intensity of the feeling rated on a scale from 0 to 10, with ten being the worst or most difficult. For example, if you would like to release resentment towards your first-grade best friend who left town and abandoned you, it might feel like a 2 or 3 feeling. If you would like to overcome abuse, the loss of a family member, or something more traumatic, you might have a feeling that rates between an 8 and 10.

This step aims to help you monitor your progress after performing a complete EFT round or sequence and identify how many more sequences you need to conduct to heal from a situation. If your initial intensity was ten before tapping and ended at 5, you would have accomplished a 50 percent improvement.

3. The third step is establishing a phrase explaining the situation or issue. It must focus on two main goals: acknowledging the issue and loving/accepting yourself despite the problem. The common setup phrase is: "Even though I have this [issue or feeling], I deeply and completely love and accept myself." You can change the phrase to fit your problem and feel right for you, but it is important to focus on how the situation makes you feel so the distress it causes can be relieved. It is also important not to skip the self-loving and self-acceptance part at the end. It is crucial to tell our subconscious mind that we are loved and accepted despite our emotions or what happened to us.

Now that you identified the issue and have a phrase to explain it, you can start with the first tapping sequence.
The EFT tapping sequence is the methodic tapping on the ends of nine meridian points.

- Karate chop (KC): small intestine meridia
- Top of the head (TH): governing vessel
- Eyebrow (EB): bladder meridian
- Side of the eye (SE): gallbladder meridian
- Under the eye (UE): stomach meridian
- Under the nose (UN): governing vessel
- Chin (Ch): central vessel
- Beginning of the collarbone (CB): kidney meridian
- Under the arm (UA): spleen meridian

Begin by tapping the karate chop point while simultaneously reciting your setup phrase three times. Then, tap each following point five to seven times, moving down the body in this ascending order: eyebrow, side of the eye, under the eye, under the nose, chin, beginning of the collarbone, under the arm.

After tapping the underarm point, you finish the sequence by tapping both of the insides of your wrists together, and I like to recite the setup phrase again to close the sequence.

While tapping the ascending points, you don't have to continue with the setup phrase, but ensure that you choose reminder phrases that help you remain focused on your problem area. If your setup phrase is, "Even though I feel resentment towards my childhood friend, I deeply and completely accept myself," your reminder phrase can be, "The resentment I feel," or "Even though I am still hurt," etc. The important thing is to always focus on the issue to ensure energy release.

You can go through all the points two or three times or until it feels right, and the last step would be to test the final intensity of the emotion. At the end of your sequence, rate your intensity level on a scale of 0 to 10 and compare your results with your initial intensity level. Depending on the issue and the progress made, you could release a negative emotion or energy blockage after 3 or 4 sequences. For more traumatic events, it might take longer. If the instructions were difficult to follow or you would like to see some examples, I encourage you to look for YouTube videos. There are thousands of free resources you can learn from and follow to apply EFT Tapping to your own situation.

As you can see, this Tapping technique is also an amazing self-love technique. You can also use it to boost your confidence, reduce stress levels, and clear an overactive mind. The primary thing you need to do is to change the setup phrase and additional affirmations to suit the situation you want to release.

Meditation/Visualization

Meditation and Visualization are also amazing techniques we can use to clear energy blockages and remove negative emotions from our emotional bodies.

There is a broad spectrum of meditation options, and you can choose any meditation approach that resonates with you. If you are new to meditation, I recommend looking for a guided healing meditation video on YouTube. You can try different ones and choose one that resonates with you and feels right.

If you are a spiritual person, a meditation that involves asking your divinity or the universe to help you release negative emotions and heal your wounds is also extremely powerful. Visualize white light everywhere around you and the angels healing the body part you feel is storing the emotion. In this type of meditation, the most important part is your faith in having this done.

Visualization can also help rewrite memories from difficult situations or traumatic experiences. You can visualize the situation and try to remember what happened. Feel what you felt at that particular time. And then change the outcome in your visualization to a positive one. It is like rewriting your past and has very powerful results. Use your imagination and visualize an outcome that makes you feel good.

For example, suppose you were the victim of bullying at school. In that case, you can imagine defending yourself and the bullies suddenly asking for your forgiveness and leaving you alone, or a teacher, a friend, or your adult self coming to the scene and protecting you from the bullies.

After doing that a couple of times, you won't even remember the initial situation, and the negative feelings associated with that particular situation will be gone. When you recall that part of your life, you will probably remember the outcome you imagined instead of what happened.

You can use this technique together with EFT Tapping for more powerful results. After a tapping sequence, visualize the situation with your new outcome.

I have used these two techniques to heal from some very traumatic experiences and can comfortably tell you that whenever I recall what happened, my positive outcome is what I remember; I no longer have an associated negative emotion. Even if I try hard to remember what actually happened, there is no longer a negative feeling involved.

Hypnosis

After EFT Tapping, Hypnosis was the second most effective tool I used to get over traumatic experiences in my life. I used guided self-hypnosis videos I found on YouTube, and they made all the difference; if I found these videos so helpful, I can only imagine what a session with a therapist would do.

Hypnosis helps you reach your subconscious mind and solve issues directly at the source. If you have had a very traumatic experience that you cannot remember or if it is hard to deal with something because of how painful it was, hypnotherapy sessions can be the best healing technique because our conscious mind does not necessarily need to be involved in the process.

I was asleep through most of the guided hypnosis meditations I did, and they worked very well. How do I know? Because I can tell you that the next day I woke up feeling like a completely different person.

Hypnotherapy helped me calm an overactive mind, heal unresolved issues, and forgive people that hurt me. It has also helped me feel more confident and have a better sense of self, so I recommend it to everyone —you should try it, even if just once. You can do it for free using free videos, which is what I did, or visit a licensed therapist; either way, after some weeks, I can assure you that your life will completely change.

Inner child healing

One of my favorite healing methods has to be inner child work or reparenting the inner child. The inner child is the most sensitive and vulnerable side of our personalities. It forms in the first years of our lives, usually influenced by the positive and negative experiences we had as children. Depending on our life experiences, our inner child can store more positive or negative traits in our subconscious mind.

However, our inner child traits come out as adults when we are dealing with difficult or stressful situations or when we have a similar traumatic experience we lived as a child. Our inner child also determines how we react to certain circumstances, especially if our wounds are deep. Therefore, it is very important to heal our inner child, so we can overcome those deep wounds from our childhood and let go of the negative emotions that are like a heavy burden on our shoulders.

There are many different techniques for inner child work. The techniques mentioned above can also work for inner child healing; you just need to readapt them for this specific goal.

To start healing the inner child, it is important to list the traumatic and difficult events you experienced in your childhood. Everything that caused you pain, no matter how big or small the situation was. I like to do it in chronological order to ensure that I don't forget any part of my life. For example:

1. "I felt hurt when my second-grade best friend stopped talking to me."

2. "My grandpa died when I was 4, which was very traumatic."

3. "My best friend changed me for another person, and I felt betrayed."

And so on:
There will be some events that we shall struggle to recall because of how painful they were. In those cases, you can use meditation to recall traumatic events in your childhood, and you will probably get a hint or remember what happened. Either look for a guided meditation on YouTube or sit down and focus on your breath with a resolute intention to recall childhood memories that need acknowledging.

When the list is ready, you should go through every event individually, trying your best to recall what happened, who was involved, and how you felt at that moment. Then, you can use one of the mentioned techniques to process the negative emotions and let go of the situation. Depending on how deep a wound goes, one technique might work better than another.

For example, if you have dealt with abuse or bullying or have feelings of shame and guilt, EFT Tapping is a powerful technique you can use to release the energy of those emotions. If you felt betrayed by someone, meditation and visualization might help you forgive the person and change the memory.

After working on healing the inner child and releasing the negative emotions, take some time to nurture your inner child by giving her some love. Imagine you are your mother or father, and do/say what you would have wanted to hear/get from your parents as a child. Give your inner child love, attention, validation, and lots of mental hugs.

If other people involved caused you pain, I recommend dedicating time to working on forgiving them. Forgiveness is an extremely important step in the healing process, if not the most important one. Forgiving doesn't mean we agree with the actions of the person who hurt us or even that we want to continue having a relationship with them. It means we are ready to let go of the situation. By forgiving, we help ourselves because we remove the energy of that person and situation from our lives, so we can heal and move on. So, after each point on the list, take some time to forgive the person involved and yourself.

To forgive, you can also use the Ho'oponopono technique, a Hawaiian practice for reconciliation and forgiveness. It consists of four steps: Repentance, Forgiveness, Gratitude, and Love, and it is a very powerful way to heal and let go -not only of people but also situations.

The most common phrases used in this method are "I'm sorry," "I forgive you," "Thank you," and "I love you," but you can adjust them for your specific situation or person.

I practice Ho'oponopono by sitting in a meditation pose and breathing deeply. Then I close my eyes and start remembering the situation or person that caused me pain.

I visualize the person in front of me and send them love from my heart. Then, I imagine conversing with them, telling them what happened and how that made me feel.

When I feel I said everything I wanted to say to that person, I repeat the following phrases three times: "I'm sorry," "I forgive you," "Thank you," and "I love you." Then I visualize a bubble of pink light surrounding the person and taking them away, cutting the energetic cord connecting us in that particular situation.

This practice is extremely healing because it helps us become more compassionate towards ourselves and others. It also helps improve our relationships because we can see tangible results after we practice Ho'oponopono with people we know.

When you finish going through your list, which might take some days, weeks, or even months, try to establish a regular practice of nurturing your inner child.

Now and then, you can visualize talking to your inner child, playing, or giving him/her some attention and love. You could also do some of the things you loved as a child or go to places you have always wanted to go (like Disneyland or camping). When your inner child is happy, it won't be easy to trigger you, and you will become less reactive and more emotionally stable.

Journaling

Journaling is a well-known therapeutic technique that helps us process feelings and emotions by putting them on paper. When we write down what happened, we organize our ideas and can see things and situations from different perspectives. I have found it especially helpful to let go of events that happened to me that were so painful that I couldn't concentrate on them using EFT Tapping or meditation. The emotion was gone, but I would continue thinking about what happened, trying to make sense of it, but it was neither helpful nor healthy for my healing.

By writing down what happened, what we think about it, and how we felt, we feel relief and rise above the situation and see it through different lenses. It's like talking to a therapist or a good friend without the urge to censure some things.

There are several ways you can approach this method. You can write a letter to yourself and explain everything as if you were a friend. Write everything that comes to mind about a situation or your current feelings without paying attention to be coherent or have a cohesive text. Simply let the feelings flow while you write them down. You could also write it like a story in the third person to help you separate from the situation and see it with different eyes as if you were writing a book about it. There is no right or wrong way to use journaling. Use your intuition and do what feels right for you and motivates you.

You could also create a habit out of it and do it regularly. Creating a journaling practice can be a life-changing way to learn to process emotions, listen to our feelings, and honor our progress.

Another option is to write down everything you want to release, burn what you write, and then ask the universe to take away all the negative feelings and emotions so you can heal from them.

Regardless of which method you decide to use, the action of putting your thoughts on paper will help release the situation and let it go.

Therapy

If you feel like you have tried everything suggested but aren't seeing a lot of progress or you feel stuck, consider working with a psychotherapist. Therapy is one of the best investments you can give yourself and one of the best tools for self-improvement.

If you are considering therapy, I recommend not settling for any therapist unless you are 100% sure it is the right fit and feels right for you. Your intuition is particularly important as you choose the right therapist for your situation.

Working with a psychotherapist can be one of the best things you can do to heal your wounds and let go of the past. It can also help you identify the coping mechanisms you created to deal with difficult situations that are now blocking you in your adult life. Therapy can also illuminate some of the negative beliefs you inherited from your parents or created in your early years that are causing you to remain stuck in negative patterns that hinder your ability to create the life you want.

Although I believe everyone can heal themselves, therapy can be a faster and more effective way of identifying the psychological blockages and wounds stored in our subconscious minds and how to get rid of them.

You can use many other practices to heal yourself and release the negative emotions and feelings related to your past, but I wanted to talk about the ones that have worked for me after a lot of trial and error. However, please research some more; you might find techniques that work better for you and your situation.

After finding a technique that works best for you, stick with it! The healing journey might take a few days, months, or a few years, and we never really stop healing. There are always new situations in our lives that can wound us, and practicing these healing techniques regularly can help you overcome obstacles more easily.

What a journey, right? I think this step is one of the most difficult and life-changing ones of them all. It might take you longer than expected, and you might continue reading this book without fully healing all your wounds, but that is ok. The truth is that healing our past is hard work. Some of us have gathered negative emotions for decades without taking the time to process and heal them. See this as a journey instead of a one-day step.

It took me around four years to start clearing the baggage I was carrying from my past, to identify the blockages I had, and to heal my inner child. And there are still some situations I haven't fully healed from, and I know it will take some more time. But I now feel lighter and happier because of everything I have achieved so far. So, be patient with yourself and enjoy the journey. And focus on your achievements and how much you learn in the process.

You probably feel much lighter, happier, and more optimistic by now. And your life has been turned upside down, hasn't it? You have released so much that you are probably finding more time and space to do things you love doing.

You have also made peace with your past and forgiven people that hurt you. And you probably realized that everything that has happened to you until now has made you wiser and stronger. Now it is time to release the negative self-talk, feelings of not being enough, and limiting beliefs that hinder you from living your best life.

Step 5: Identify Negative Beliefs

The last step in this section is to identify the negative narrative that has been playing in our heads and kept us stuck in our low self-esteem and negative thinking.

Though you don't realize it, thousands of thoughts run through your head during the day, like a record playing in the background. These thoughts have a huge impact on your life. If you have negative self-talk and are always judging yourself, the chances are high that you also have low self-esteem. The problem is that our actions are also aligned with those negative thoughts and don't allow us to progress in life and reach our highest potential.

How would you feel if someone criticized you all day long? You would probably feel down, not good enough, and doubtful of your capacities, right? The funny thing is that we do it to ourselves all day long without even realizing it. And we are sometimes so cruel that we say things we wouldn't even dare to say to someone else.

This negative self-talk only holds us back, keeping us stuck in a negative spiral, which is why it is so important to identify and change the narrative. When we look at ourselves differently, with radical love and acceptance, we also increase our confidence, self-esteem, and self-worth. We feel worthy and capable of anything we set our minds to do and don't hesitate to work towards our goals and dreams.

How to identify negative beliefs

One of the most successful ways to identify this internal narrative is meditation. Meditation allows us to calm our minds and gain awareness of the thoughts that enter our minds. Meditating, even for five minutes a day, trains us to be observers of our realities and gain a different perspective toward our actions, thoughts, and emotions. We begin to notice our thought patterns, limiting beliefs, and the tone of the internal narrative we have going on. Introspection also brings to the surface the emotions that haven't been processed and allows us to work on them and release them.

Although there are many types of meditation, the most common is focusing our awareness on the breath or another body sensation. Every time our mind wanders, we acknowledge the thought that popped up, let it go, and refocus our awareness on our breath.

At first, concentrating on the breath can be difficult because we are used to "thinking" all the time. Especially if you are a worrier like me, you would think of all the possible things that could go wrong at a given moment or situation, and when you start to meditate, it is a challenge to focus on your breath for a second. However, practice makes it easier, and the mind learns to calm itself down the more we meditate.

To start identifying the internal narrative, it is important to acknowledge the nature of the thoughts that pop up while you meditate. You would be amazed to see how cruel you are to yourself and how many of your thoughts relate to fear, criticism, and/or irrational worries. It is usually hard to change our lifestyle and go after our goals and dreams if we constantly inflict fear on ourselves.

The longer we practice meditation, the easier it gets to become an observer of our internal narrative during the day while performing other activities or talking to other people. This allows us to stop ourselves from self-criticism, worrying, and creating negative scenarios in our minds, whether it is during a meditative state or not. This also helps us control our feelings and be more conscious of what we do and say to others.

If focusing on your breath is a type of meditation you don't like or it doesn't work for you, consider practicing meditation by identifying your thoughts during different meditative activities like playing an instrument or going for a walk.

The important thing is that you are present in the moment and identify the thoughts that pop up, which will make you aware of how you speak to yourself, your fears, and the thoughts holding you back from reaching your highest potential.

Apart from the negative narrative and self-criticism, it is important to identify the limiting beliefs that hold us back. Growing up, we adopt limiting beliefs from the people around us, especially our parents. If we grow up in a family with issues around money, we might have adopted the belief that we will never have financial abundance. If our parents had a difficult relationship, we might have adopted the belief that love doesn't exist or that we are not deserving of love. If we experience physical or emotional abuse, we may believe we are not good enough, there is something wrong with us, or we do not deserve true love.

We all have limiting beliefs in different areas of our lives, some of which keep us from reaching our goals and following our dreams. And even if we do, we would sabotage ourselves because our subconscious mind would convince us that we don't deserve success, love, or happiness.

Growing up, I had everything I needed and was privileged compared to most people in the world, but we didn't have extra money to spend. We always had a place to live, new clothes, food on our table, and the chance to receive a good education. However, my parents had a negative relationship with money and limiting beliefs around it. They always felt poor and like they couldn't have the life they wanted because of a lack of money.

Although I understand why they thought that way, I now realize that their apprehension towards money only made them live in fear and even block the flow of abundance. It also made me adopt the limiting belief that I couldn't have enough and that people with money probably had it because they were born rich.

Those limiting beliefs caused me to make decisions that misaligned with who I am or what I truly wanted. I would stay at a job I hated because I was afraid of losing my income, and I wouldn't dare to accept that the kind of work environment I chose was not for me, no matter how depressed and frustrated I was. I had to lose the job I hated to realize my limiting belief was holding me back.

When I understood this and replaced the belief that money is scarce and my dream job would never be a source of steady income with the belief that I deserve abundance and that what I enjoy doing can bring me that abundance, I found a perfect job for me. Now I work in an artistic environment with great colleagues and I love what I do.

We don't realize how many limiting beliefs we have regarding different areas of our lives until we start doing some inner work and digging a little deeper. That is why it is so important to identify them and start changing them so they stop having control over our lives.

The best way to identify these beliefs is to listen to your inner narrative and all the times you use the word "but."

For example, "I would like to learn this, but," "I would love to have my own business, but," or "I feel I should be doing XZY, but..."

All those "but" have a root in a limiting belief that keeps us from building the life we want. Whenever you hear a "but" in your head, analyze where it is coming from and identify the underlying limiting belief.

Another way to identify these beliefs is to pay attention to what goes wrong when you are about to achieve something you want or when you have relationship problems with someone who truly loves you. If you are honest with yourself and understand the root of the issue, you will probably find a negative belief that manifests the problem. Maybe you met someone who loves you, but you feel unworthy and undeserving of love. Your subconscious mind will start sabotaging your relationship by creating discussions and problems around silly things until you break up with the person. Or if you start a business but don't feel good enough, you will make bad decisions to sabotage your business's success because deep inside, you don't feel you deserve to be successful. By analyzing the distressing situations in your life, you will identify some of the limiting beliefs holding you back.

You can also identify limiting beliefs by analyzing the areas you are unhappy with and digging deep to find your beliefs in that area. For example, if you are unhappy with being single and find it hard to find a partner that loves you unconditionally, you might believe you don't deserve love, or that love doesn't exist.

Once you identify this internal narrative and limiting beliefs, it is important to stop and then change them. Stopping the negative thoughts will momentarily help you gain control over what you say to yourself, but it doesn't assure you these thoughts won't pop up again a few minutes, hours, or days later. After all, they are messages sent by your subconscious mind that reflect how you feel inside and how your self-esteem levels are.

Therefore, to completely transform your life, you need to change the narrative to a new one that encourages you, helps you value yourself more, and realize how beautiful and talented you are.

The first step to stopping negative self-talk or letting go of a limiting belief is challenging it. Analyze where it came from and identify if it was something you adopted from someone else or a belief you created because of an experience you had. When you realize that the belief is not even yours in the first place, it is easier to challenge and refuse it.

In my case, I realized that my beliefs around money were not mine but something I picked up from my parents. That helped me challenge them by looking for examples that would prove those beliefs wrong. I started learning about people who built successful businesses from the ground, those who earn a lot of money from doing what they love, and other examples that proved my belief wrong. By doing that exercise, I convinced myself that the belief I had adopted was false and was not serving me, so I refused it and let it go.

The same process applies to beliefs or thought patterns you created because of a negative experience.

After surviving bullying, my self-esteem was at its lowest, and I believed something was wrong with me. It took me some time to identify this, but when I did, I started challenging it with positive affirmations and rebuilding my self-image. I got to know myself better, the good and the bad, and realized that we are all worthy and valuable just the way we are.

It is very important to identify and release negative beliefs and thought patterns because they also create our experiences. Our subconscious mind filters information to our conscious mind according to our beliefs. For example, if you think the world is difficult, your subconscious mind will ensure it filters the information that matches that belief. Therefore, you will see news, meet people and have experiences that support the belief that life is difficult. For that reason, a very important step to changing your life is to release the limiting beliefs holding you back.

In the next part of the book, I will give you some useful techniques you can use to transform those negative beliefs into positive ones.

Part 3: How to Rebuild Your Life

If you are reading this, it means you followed my previous steps and let go of everything that wasn't serving you. You have let go of all the clutter you had at home, the negative relationships that have held you back, the negative habits that kept you on the downward spiral, and your limiting beliefs. You might be feeling like a completely different person already.

At this stage, you may find that the things and activities you used to love are no longer as enjoyable, and you can also feel lonely. It is very common that after a big change in our lives, the people around us either don't resonate with us anymore or are shocked by seeing us evolve into different people. So it can feel like a lonely process if our support system isn't very strong already. But the positive side is that now you have more time to get to know yourself and find who you truly are.

We often think we know who we are. We say, "I am a mother," "I am a lawyer," "I am a good friend," and "I am intelligent," but all those words are just describing our physical appearance, the social role we play, our sexual orientation, or our profession. However, that is not who we are. We are so much more than that.

I believe we are multifaceted spiritual beings or souls living a human experience. We all come to this world with weaknesses and strengths that we use or work on throughout our lives to learn lessons and fulfill our purpose. That is what makes us unique and special.

Through the first five steps of this book, I guided you to release everything that doesn't serve you so you can find who you truly are. You probably identified the things you like to have around you, what you like to do, and the people you want to have in your life. And if none of the above is true, at least you know what aligns with what you want. From this point on, I will guide you to start building the life you want.

The sixth step involves reprogramming your mind to ensure you have a positive attitude toward yourself and the confidence to reach your goals.

We normally have many limiting beliefs about ourselves and the world we inherited from our parents or built during childhood. As the name implies, these limiting beliefs set a limit to our dreams and achievements and don't allow us to build an abundant and prosperous life. That is why it is very important to identify and change those limiting beliefs, so you can stop self-sabotage and start allowing abundance into your life.

The seventh step is to be aware of your emotions and "shadow self." We all have a "shadow" or a part of our personality that we are unaware of or don't want to accept. It is usually in our subconscious mind and appears in the form of instinctive behavior.

When you integrate your shadows, you become complete and acknowledge that even though parts of you may look negative or as a weakness, they are still part of you and important. Being aware of your shadow allows you to stop reacting to triggering situations and instead respond consciously.

The eighth step will show you how to build positive habits that help you live a more balanced and harmonious life. You have probably already started one or two positive habits to release old negative habits or addictions that were holding you back. Now, you can consciously create new healthy and productive habits that are a stepping stone to achieving your goals and creating the life you desire.

The next step involves building new meaningful relationships that encourage you to grow and improve. This is a lifetime process, but we will focus on building a strong relationship with ourselves. We are normally not aware that our internal reality mirrors our external reality. Thus, to create solid, stable, and loving relationships, we must first build one with ourselves.

Lastly, you can relax and enjoy the hard work by adapting your space to the new you and have some fun remodeling your personal space and wardrobe. I will give you my tips on how to find your personal style so you always wear what you love, feel confident every day, and keep a curated and clutter-free space. And believe me, if you still haven't noticed how you have changed, you will not recognize yourself by the end of this chapter.

Step 6: Reset Your Thoughts

In step 5, I helped you identify the negative narrative and limiting beliefs playing like a broken record in your subconscious mind. You have probably realized how cruel you were towards yourself and how many limiting beliefs had blocked your progress and success or damaged you physically, mentally, or emotionally.

However, how do you get rid of them? The first step is acknowledging them, so you are already on the right path. The next step is rewriting that internal narrative. Since you have been carrying those thoughts and beliefs for decades, probably since you were very young, your subconscious mind will not easily let them go. To change the narrative, we need to rewrite it.

Our subconscious mind works differently than our conscious mind and is not so easy to access, so rationally trying to change the thoughts does not really work, or at least not so effectively. The best way to rewrite your subconscious mind is to use a method to access it directly to ensure you can have direct communication with it. During my self-discovery process, I used different methods to rewrite my internal narrative, but the ones that showed the best results were the following.

EFT Tapping

I introduced this method in step four and explained how you could tap on some meridian points in your body to release negative emotions stored in your body from past trauma. Well, since this method helps you engage and directly communicate with your subconscious mind, you can also use it to rewrite your internal narrative.

Here, you first need to choose some positive affirmations opposite to the negative ones you recognized. For example, if you tell yourself, "I can't do anything right," you could say, "I always do the right thing," or "I always make the best decision." If you don't feel good enough, you can say, "I am enough." It doesn't matter if you don't feel it is true as you are saying it or if it feels strange to do it; your subconscious mind will still get the message.

Positive Affirmations

Like EFT Tapping, you can use positive affirmations to reprogram your subconscious mind.

You can say affirmations to yourself while looking in the mirror in the morning, listen to them from a YouTube video, or record your voice and play them in your car, commute, or before going to bed. Hearing positive affirmations in your voice or from a video will send the message directly to your subconscious mind. Over time, this will overwrite/rewrite the negative narrative.

This has been a truly life-changing method for me. I remember how uncomfortable I felt when I first started repeating positive affirmations and didn't believe what I was telling myself. In contrast, now I look in the mirror and immediately see a beautiful person in front of me and feel deep love and appreciation for myself.

Hypnosis

Hypnotherapy is a great way to reach your subconscious mind without engaging your conscious mind. Once in a hypnotic state, you can directly communicate with your subconscious without your ego blocking the connection with fear-based feelings.

You can work with a hypnotherapist to rewrite the negative narrative, listen to self-hypnosis videos or audio clips on YouTube or Spotify, or get into a hypnotic state during meditation and listen to positive affirmations

while in that state. Hypnosis is also a great technique if you haven't managed to incorporate EFT or other positive affirmations into your daily routine.

My preferred way is guided hypnosis meditation videos on YouTube mainly because you can choose hypnosis for self-love, abundance, or whatever you want to improve and listen to them before sleep. I normally fall asleep after a few minutes, but I continue listening to the session anyway, and I find that better because my conscious mind doesn't interfere with the message. The next morning I wake up feeling more confident, loved, and connected. This technique has improved my self-esteem and self-worth and opened me up for abundance and success.

If you try incorporating one of these techniques into your daily routine, you will soon see changes in how you treat yourself and how others treat you. We don't realize that the people around us are mirrors of what we feel inside, so if we say negative things to ourselves all the time, the people in our environment will do too. And it is an immediate shift. I remember starting to say my daily affirmations for a couple of weeks, and people around me would tell me the same things I was telling myself. If I said, "I am strong," someone would compliment me saying how strong I was. It is that literal.

Working with positive affirmations doesn't only help rewrite the internal narrative; it also helps you develop a more stable sense of self-esteem and self-worth. It can help us start treating ourselves better, care more for our bodies, and treat other people and animals better. And that has an immense impact on our lives in general.

We can also use these techniques to rewrite limiting beliefs about money, wealth, success, love, and other things we think we don't deserve. If you think you cannot live the life you want because you don't have money, start saying, "I am rich," "I have material abundance," "I am wealthy," or "Money flows naturally to me." If you think you will never find a partner, change the narrative to "I am open for love" and "I deserve love." You can truly change any limiting belief by substituting it for a new uplifting one.

And to permanently change your negative beliefs, you have to choose to make a different decision and stop the pattern related to that belief. For example, if you think love doesn't exist and you meet someone new, instead of consciously or subconsciously trying to sabotage the relationship, choose to give the person a chance and remind yourself that love does exist and you are worthy of it.

When you decide to act differently and stop listening to the limiting belief, you tell your subconscious mind that your belief has changed because you have replaced it accordingly.

This step might be one of the most transformational ones in this book because it is the one that will show the biggest results. Opening yourself to releasing all detrimental thought patterns and beliefs will truly change your life.

Positive affirmations profoundly affected my life. After being an anxious person with very low self-esteem and attracting toxic and abusive people, I became confident and sure of myself. I felt worthy of love, joy, and abundance. The people around me started treating me better, and I no longer sabotaged myself from achieving success.

Step 7: Be Aware of Your Emotions

In step four, you went on a self-discovery journey to find all the negative emotions you were still carrying from your past; you also learned how to release them.

It is amazing how much freedom this process can give us. I bet you feel lighter and happier. And even though it is not an easy thing to do, you managed to face those past traumas and heal them.

It is now time to face your shadow. The "shadow" is a concept coined by Carl Jung. It refers to the aspects of our personality we choose to reject, repress, or are simply not consciously aware of. They are all the parts of ourselves that we don't like or don't accept, so we hide them in our subconscious minds.

Every one of us has a shadow self because it is the part of us that makes us react impulsively when triggered by someone or something. The shadow can be aggressive impulses, shameful experiences, fears, or irrational wishes. To control these impulses, we must integrate the shadow part into our personality, face the parts of ourselves we are rejecting or repressing, and accept them.

When we accept our shadow self, even if we feel uncomfortable with some aspects of its personality traits, we "bring it to the light." We become conscious of it, which denies it control over us. We become whole again and consciously choose how to respond in any given situation because we will no longer be triggered.

I want to highlight that there is nothing inherently positive or negative about the traits and characteristics we have in our shadow, or even the ones we are already aware of. They become negative when we act unconsciously from that place and hurt ourselves and others.

I believe shadow work is necessary for self-healing and is a lifetime journey and process. Doing shadow work helps us release feelings of shame and face our fears, be more accepting of ourselves and others, and be more confident in ourselves. The more we face our shadow aspects and accept them, the more authentic we can be. And also accept the authenticity of others as we become less judgmental and more open to different types of people.

Although it sounds scary, shadow work doesn't have to be difficult. The most important step is to be open to accepting those parts of our personality and stop being judgmental about them. Since these parts of our personality are suppressed deeply in our subconscious, there are several methods you can use to become aware of them.

Projection

The first method you can use is to acknowledge how you project your shadow onto other people. If you tend to judge or criticize others, especially on an impulse, you are projecting part of your shadow onto that person.

If someone says something silly and you react by saying, "he is so stupid," there is probably a silly side shadow you haven't recognized or accepted. If you criticize how someone else dresses, you probably feel insecure that you might be criticized for what you wear and thus do it to another person to "reassure" yourself that you wouldn't take the risk to dress how you truly want.

Everything we don't like in another person comes from a shadow part of us that we haven't accepted, something we haven't accepted about ourselves. And this is also true for the things we admire in others or are jealous of. If you admire a friend for his discipline, it means you also have that ability in you; you just haven't discovered it or worked on it yet. When you feel jealous of how a coworker gives presentations without feeling nervous, it is because you are also good at presenting to others but might be scared to try it out.

Identifying what we project onto others gives us a clue about what things are part of us but that we haven't accepted or discovered, including both negative and positive aspects. So I invite you to be more conscious of what you criticize or admire in others and realize how your shadow might be projecting.

Character identification

We do more than project our shadow onto other people; we also do it with characters in movies, TV shows, and novels.

It is common to identify with someone specific in a movie or to hate or dislike a character. When we have strong feelings towards a character, it is probably our shadow projecting some aspects of ourselves.

Consider an example where you always like the heroine in a movie because of her bravery, strong personality, ideals, courage, and discipline. You feel that because you have the same personality traits, but they are probably hiding in your shadow.

The same happens when you hate the villain. Thinking about the fictional characters we have strong feelings towards can allow us to see different aspects of ourselves we need to integrate.

These two methods are good starting points to begin doing shadow work by looking at our own reflection in the face of other people. When you have an idea of the personality aspects, fears, or feelings you might be suppressing in your subconscious mind, you can easily integrate those shadow parts by accepting them.

Conscious awareness and acceptance mean they are no longer hiding and that even though you might not like some of them, you accept that they are part of you and have chosen not to develop them or let them control you. And the ones you like, you can develop and enhance so you become the best version of yourself.

And to completely integrate your shadow, you have to choose to act differently every time a shadow aspect arises. It might be difficult at first, because we have been running the same patterns for years, or sometimes decades. But it is a matter of becoming more aware of our thoughts and actions and choose what is aligned with our values and the person we want to be.

After the bullying I suffered at work, I remember hating the person who started the smear campaign. I had deep negative feelings towards him and thought he was a liar, dishonest, and a hypocritical person.

During my recovery, I took some time to face my own shadow and realized I hated him so much because those were traits I also had in myself, and I subconsciously also behaved that way sometimes. I did not do it to the extent of hurting another person, but I would sometimes lie about my opinions so other people would like me. I would pretend I liked someone to avoid conflict, and I was not honest with myself about what I wanted.

Once I accepted those aspects of myself, I consciously chose to change them. I stopped every type of lie, even if they were those "white lies" accepted by society. I started to be more honest with myself and others, even if it meant I needed to face conflict. Doing that also allowed me to become a more authentic version of myself.

And remember, it is not about judging. The moment we accept and love those parts of ourselves that we suppressed, we start to love and cherish ourselves more. And our compassion towards others grows as well.

When doing shadow work, it is very common for negative emotions to surface. We may feel guilt or shame for our behaviors, or pain because of things that happened in the past. Therefore, it is very important to release these emotions when they surface. That is why I want to teach you how to release emotions when they appear to ensure you don't build heavy baggage again. You can use this to release the emotions that surface during shadow work and daily life.

In his book **Letting Go,** Dr. David Hawkins explains how we normally either suppress, repress or express emotions, but none of those coping mechanisms are helpful. When we suppress our feelings, it means it is so shocking to us that we are unconscious of the emotion and just store it in our subconscious mind. That is very common, especially in childhood, when we don't normally have the tools to cope with or process traumatic events. This is something we do a lot to deal with traumatic or difficult experiences.

In my early twenties, one of my friends (or someone I thought was my friend) deeply hurt me. Out of extreme shock over what happened, I didn't even think much about it. Instead, I suppressed the emotion in my subconscious. I remember just going about my day like nothing had happened and even continuing the friendship with the person.

At that time, I thought it hadn't affected me, but after some time, the memory of what happened and the associated emotions resurfaced, and the pain was real. I also realized that I had been carrying that emotion and pain for a long time, and it was hurting me, even if I wasn't consciously aware of it.

The same happens when we repress emotions. Repressing emotions mean we consciously decide not to deal with them. It is there, but we look for various forms of distraction to ensure we don't have to face the emotion. This also means we are carrying a burden that doesn't allow us to feel free or experience joy. It is very common to repress feelings like guilt or jealousy because we feel shame for experiencing them. But the more we repress an emotion, the longer it holds us back and keeps us trapped.

We normally think expressing emotions is the best way to deal with them. That is actually how psychoanalysis and other forms of psychotherapy work. However, Dr. Hawkins explains that when we express emotion, we re-live the negative situation and only release a part of it. Talking about what happened doesn't mean the emotion will go away.

The only way to truly face and let go of our negative emotions is to surrender to them. Experience the pain and consciously release everything. We can do this by allowing the emotion or pain to take over our bodies and just observing that emotion. We must also acknowledge the feelings and sensations we experience and relax our bodies.

Emotions are how our subconscious mind communicates with us. They tell us that there is an unresolved issue that we need to solve. When we face a negative emotion, it no longer has a purpose for existing, and we release it.

It can also help to see things from a different, higher perspective and rise above the situation. For example, when facing feelings of guilt, we can see how the situation was there to help us grow and forgive ourselves. If it is anger, we can be more compassionate towards the person and understand why the person might have acted in a certain way. We can always learn a lesson, even in the most painful experiences. And when we learn the lesson, there is also no longer a reason for the emotion, so we release it.

Now that you know how to integrate your shadow and let go of emotions, you can feel more in control of how you respond to different situations in your life. It is less likely you will be triggered by others, and even if you are, you now know it is because there is something you still need to work on.

You have the power to act from a conscious place and decide not to be emotionally affected by a situation. And you can choose to release the emotions right away instead of holding on to them.

The truth is that we will always feel different emotions, positive and negative, it is part of the human experience. Our power lies in consciously deciding what to do with them. And if we decide to listen to what they have to say and learn the lesson, there is not need for them to stay with us and hold us down.

Step 8: Acquire New Positive Habits

Since we have already covered some of this part in step 3, you have probably started some new habits as replacements for negative ones. Maybe you started an exercise routine, a new hobby, or a healthy eating habit. In this step, I invite you to consciously decide to incorporate some new positive habits into your life according to what you want.

Habits are stronger than we realize because they shape our lives. Our brains get used to them and become more and more automatic with time, requiring less effort each time. More than 40 percent of our daily actions are habits, not decisions. That is why they can be very positive or very detrimental.

They work through the habit loop, which means there is a cue or trigger that initiates it, a routine, and a reward. Because there is a reward, the habit loop is reinforced, becoming automatic over time.

An example of a habit loop would be: We go to the gym, and that specific location triggers us to exercise, which is the routine. After exercise, the pleasure chemicals released in the brain are the reward.

You have probably heard that it takes 21 days to create a habit. However, depending on the type of habit, it can take longer. Therefore, the most important aspect of creating a new habit is consistency.

If you are determined to program your brain to perform the routine automatically when the cue or trigger occurs, you must reinforce it several times. Therefore, committing to the new habit and being consistent is the key to making it part of your life without effort.

For example, to improve your productivity, you could create habits like waking up earlier, keeping a journal, or creating a morning routine. If your goal is to improve your health, you could focus on healthy eating habits, learn how to cook, or start an exercise program. Positive affirmations and self-care habits are best for you if you want to be more confident.

The habit change process is very individual to you because we all have different goals and aspirations. However, if I can recommend one lifelong habit you can start that will change your life, it would be to have a mindfulness or meditation practice. Meditation is an excellent way to be present and calm your mind from negative thoughts and beliefs; it also has proven health benefits for your mind, body, and soul.

You can use meditation to increase awareness, train your mind to focus and concentrate better and reduce stress and anxiety. You can also use meditation lessons to develop other beneficial habits like positive thinking, self-discipline, better sleep patterns, and tolerance to pain.

Some meditation approaches can also help us develop deeper compassion and kindness towards ourselves and others.

Meditation is an excellent way to develop self-love and increase our self-esteem. It also helps us forgive ourselves and others and let go of the unresolved issues we haven't released.

You can start a loving-kindness meditation practice to work on the emotional issues you haven't let go of using the tools I share with you in this book. It can also help you fight addiction and control food cravings, making it a great way to replace old negative patterns or addictive behaviors.

When we meditate, we deeply connect with ourselves, our soul, and that part of us that is wise and has all the answers. Sometimes, we neglect that part of ourselves because we have identified too much with our ego and our mind. That is a shame because all the answers we need lie in the part of us that speaks to us through our intuition. When we connect with that part, we learn to listen more to our intuitive nudges to make better decisions aligned with what we truly want and our purpose.

The best part is that you can do meditation anywhere and everywhere because it doesn't require equipment, tools, or special training. It is free, and you can start it anytime. You don't need to meditate for long hours to reap the beneficial results. Meditating for as little as 5 minutes a day can work wonders in your life and help you reduce stress and develop deeper self-awareness.

There are also several meditation types from which you can choose. For example, suppose you don't like focused-attention meditation types or find it very hard to concentrate. In that case, you could practice an open-monitoring meditation and be mindful of your environment, the people around you, and your thoughts and impulses. Or an active meditation like running, practicing yoga, or doing a walking meditation.

You can also choose a specific form according to your desired results, like a loving-kindness meditation to forgive, a guided meditation to connect with higher consciousness to develop your spirituality or an anxiety meditation to overcome anxiety and depression. The list is endless. The only way to find out which style suits you best is to try different exercises until you find a practice you love and can stick to for the long haul.

Personal experience has taught me that meditation is a life-changing habit. I started to meditate when I was deep in my depression and social anxiety. I read several books about overcoming social anxiety, with most listing meditation as the best tool to calm the mind and understand the negative thoughts that create fear and anxiety.

My first meditation sessions were very difficult. I was not used to being still and present, and it felt uncomfortable. But I stuck to it, doing mainly mindfulness meditations by observing the people around me during my commute or the plants and trees when walking in the park.

After some time, I became better at it. I could focus more easily and meditate for 5 minutes straight, focusing on my breath. Then I found guided meditations on YouTube that helped me visualize and connect with the universe, and they opened another world for me.

Thanks to meditation, I opened myself up to the possibility of there being something bigger than us —you can call it God, the Universe, or higher intelligence. Meditation helped me feel connected and protected. It has also given me the emotional stability I was longing for. Now, I cannot imagine going to bed without doing my meditation and connecting with my soul. No matter what new habit you want to create, you must stick to it to see the results. We can achieve anything when we focus and take action.

For example, when our bodies get used to eating healthy and exercising, we start craving healthy foods and going to the gym consistently. When we get used to waking up early, we look forward to our precious morning routine. When meditation is part of our habits, we cannot wait to have that time of connection every day.

So, my friend, create healthy habits and stick to them to make them subconscious as you move on to the next step in this transforming life guidebook.

Step 9: Build Solid Relationships

The ninth step calls on you to rebuild your social circle, but doing that requires you to develop a relationship with yourself. We normally think we know ourselves, but the truth is that very few people spend time with themselves getting to know every part of their personality, values, desires, dreams, strengths, and weaknesses.

When you ask most people a question like "Who are you?" the response is normally something like "I'm a lawyer," "I'm a mom," or "I'm an entrepreneur." While there's nothing wrong with owning such labels, the truth is that those are nothing more than job titles, roles we play in our community, or labels others put on us. They are just a part of ourselves, not who we truly are.

We also create our self-image when we grow up according to what other people think of us. We think we are how our parents, teachers, or friends told us we were and the characteristics they saw in us. But that is also not true.

Everything that others see in us is a reflection of themselves; it has nothing to do with us in reality. Just as we project parts of ourselves onto others, others project parts of themselves onto us.

When we start getting to know ourselves, we realize that most of what we thought we were is not true. The problem is that as long as we don't discover who we truly are, we cannot be our true selves either. We cannot be authentic and shine our light.

That is why I consider it so important to take the time to find out who you are at your core. You cannot start to like yourself if you don't know your talents, what you suck at, your values, or how you define success. Self-growth demands that you know what you truly want.

The path to knowing yourself better starts with spending time with yourself. Alone time is very important to connecting and being aware of all the parts that make you, well: YOU!

While working on this step, I found it helpful to document everything in a journal so I could have a complete picture of myself in the end. I recommend starting a journal and answering the following questions as honestly as possible. Take time to meditate on the answer and to think about your past and what you can remember from when you were a child.

At birth, we don't have any limitations, we are ourselves. With time, we develop a persona according to what our parents, teachers, and society wants us to be. So go back as far as you can manage and remember how you were as a kid, then answer the following questions.

- What did I love to do as a child? What were my hobbies and favorite activities?
- What was I good at? What were my talents? What did people compliment me on? In what areas did I excel?
- How was my personality? Was I introverted or more extroverted, funny or serious, loud or quiet?
- Was I usually taking the lead in my group of friends, or did I prefer to play a supportive role?
- Of what was I afraid of?
- Which things didn't I like?

Now think about yourself in the present time and ask yourself the following questions.

- What do I love doing? What are my favorite activities?
- What are my talents?

- What would I be doing now if I wasn't afraid? What would I work on if fear of failure was not part of my psyche?
- How would I dress if I didn't care what others thought?
- What are my values? What do I value most in myself and others? (i.e., honesty, authenticity, compassion, loyalty, etc.)
- What are my priorities in life? (i.e., family, friends, work, success, money)
- What are my strengths?
- What are my weaknesses? What can I improve?
- What do I want to achieve in life?
- How do I want my life to be in 5, 10, or 30 years?
- What do I love about my body? What are things I don't like about my body?
- What topics interest me at this time? What do I like to learn?
- What five words describe me?

In addition to those questions, I would highly suggest to take a personality test online. There are several of them for free and they can help you shine a light in aspects of yourself you haven't even considered. These types of tests helped me see myself with different eyes and recognize parts of myself I didn't even know I had in me.

When you complete all the questions and tests, take some time to reflect on them. I can assure you that you will discover a lot about yourself.

Knowing who we truly are and what we want helps us gain self-confidence. It helps us be sure of who we are and stop caring about what others think of us. If we know and accept our weaknesses and strengths, other people's opinions of us are not that important anymore.

The better aware we are of who we are, the higher our self-esteem. Loving and accepting all parts of ourselves unconditionally also makes it easier to love others too.

On the other hand, when we don't love ourselves, we love others from a place of lack. We give just a little of our love, feel depleted, and don't have enough love for ourselves.

Contrarily, when we love ourselves unconditionally, we love from a place of fullness; we don't have a limit to our love for ourselves; thus, we can also love others without limit. And that does more than just improve our relationships; it also helps us attract people who can give us unconditional, true love. When we love and accept ourselves, the people around us recognize the value we give ourselves and treat us accordingly.

I was amazed when I realized that the people around me who mistreated and were abusive towards me mirrored how I treated myself deep inside. My lack of self-love let them know that I wasn't valuable enough.

Mind you, I don't want to imply that abusers are not responsible for their actions or that victims cause the abuse. Not at all. I'm only saying that when we don't respect ourselves, we leave the door open for such people to enter our lives. And we don't set boundaries because we don't think we deserve more. So to improve your relationships with others and attract people who will love you unconditionally and for who you are, you first need to love and appreciate yourself completely.

Self-love is not only about loving and accepting yourself for who you are. It is also about setting boundaries when someone crosses your limits. It is saying no when you don't feel like doing something. It is about taking time to rest when you feel drained and forgiving yourself when you make a mistake.

Self-love is not just a one-moment thing; it is an everyday choice. The next section discusses self-care practices you can use to continue taking care of yourself daily.

Now that you know yourself better and understand the importance of self-love in building good stable relationships with others, it is time to start meeting new people.

If you are an introvert like me, don't worry, you don't have to push yourself to do that. But if you have begun a new hobby or exercise routine, the chances are high that you are already meeting new people. If not, you only need to be open to welcoming new relationships into your life.

In the second part of this book, you evaluated your current relationships and let go of the unsupportive ones. That means you already have a clue or idea of your relationship patterns and the type of relationships you don't want in your life.

Now take some time to think about the type of people you want in your life. How would they be? What values would they have? How would your relationship be?

Write down everything you want in your different relationships with friends, family, partners, and coworkers. Even if you aren't actively looking to meet anyone, the likelihood is high that new people will come into your life. Having a written list of the types of people you want to attract helps you focus on those aspects when you meet someone new; it also helps you be more discerning with the people you spend time with.

If you have followed the steps up to this point, you have deeply transformed. You probably have a more optimistic mindset, don't allow emotions or past situations to hold you back, and have developed unshakable self-confidence and self-esteem. When you are authentic, you also attract people who love you for who you are.

Step 10: Curate Your Personal Space

If you have made it this far, you probably feel like a completely different person, lighter, happier, and more optimistic. You know who you truly are and what you genuinely want, and you are probably taking steps to achieve your goals and dreams. Taking responsibility, facing your shadow, and releasing negative habits is not an easy task. That's why I want to take this moment to tell you how proud of you I am. You should feel proud too. Now it is time to reap the rewards of all the hard work.

After all the inner work, it is time to match your outer space with the new you- or I should say the real you, the YOU you have always been but didn't allow others to see.

On this aspect, the first thing I would like to share is how to find your personal style. Personal style, especially concerning clothes and how you decorate your personal spaces, is important because if you come to a home decorated in a way that makes you feel comfortable, inspired, and relaxed, you will likely feel amazing in that space.

We sometimes underrate the importance of surrounding ourselves with beauty and an aesthetic we like. Developing a personal style for your home and office decor can substantially improve your feelings in those spaces. How you dress is also important. Clothes and accessories are a wonderful way to express ourselves, feel more confident, and show the world a part of who we are.

Having a personal style also helps you keep a curated wardrobe, with pieces of clothing you love that go well together, which ensures you don't have an enormous closet that has nothing you want to wear. It also allows you to feel comfortable and confident with whatever you decide to wear daily. And it makes your decision- making easier in the morning, because you know that most of your clothes can mix, match, and go well together. Such a curated wardrobe is called a capsule wardrobe. I recommend you search for capsule wardrobe examples and inspiration if you are more interested, but in this section, I want you to focus on finding your personal style.

In the first step of this book, you got rid of a fair amount of possessions that were not sparking joy. The things you kept around will now give you an idea of your personal style. Start with your clothes. Look for pieces you love to wear and wear every day. If your everyday clothes are not really what you want to wear or you wear a uniform for work, think about how you would like to dress. What pieces would you love to have? You can look for inspiration on Pinterest and create your personal style board with looks that feel like you.

Your personal style doesn't have to be defined with words or be similar to someone else's. It is what you like, how you would like to look, and how you decide to express yourself. Do not take into account what others would say. Even if your style is not work-appropriate, you can still rock your favorite pieces on the weekends. The important thing is not to limit yourself.

When you have an idea of your style, assess the pieces of clothing and accessories you already have and create a list of the ones you would like to purchase. That way, you don't have to feel overwhelmed when you go to a store and see thousands of clothes that don't even match your style. Your personal style helps you focus on what you want to purchase, which helps you avoid shopping sprees where you buy on impulse and find yourself spending money on clothes you never wear.

Your shopping list doesn't need to be empty right away. Take your time to consider what you would like to have and have fun with the process of finding each piece. This is still one of my favorite ways to shop.

When I felt unfulfilled at work, I would often binge-shop. Every weekend I would go shopping and end up buying something. Most of the time, I wouldn't say I liked the clothes I bought. Some looked good on me but didn't go well with my other clothes or didn't match my personal style.

When I decided to change my life, my clothes greatly impacted the healing process. I am unsure if that is because I am a visual person who uses clothes for self-expression, but my style was the first thing I started changing that helped me with the releasing process.

When I curated my closet and built a capsule wardrobe, my life also improved. It might seem vain, but having comfortable clothes that make you feel good about yourself impacts your confidence. I now never feel I don't have anything to wear, even though I have a small wardrobe instead of hundreds of clothes. I don't spend so much time or energy deciding what to wear in the mornings, and I don't feel disappointed with my choices. I also always look and feel like myself.

I am not suggesting that you need a minimal wardrobe like me, but having a curated one with clothes that reflect your aesthetic and personal style can be a game-changer. The same applies to your furniture and decorations at home, the office, your car, and all the personal spaces where you spend your time.

We sometimes underestimate how much impact our personal spaces can have on our well-being. A clean, organized space makes you feel more comfortable and helps your mind remain calm. Surrounding yourself with beautiful decorative pieces that you love helps you feel more joyful.

Colors also have a great influence on us. If you are familiar with the psychology of color, you know that certain colors provoke certain emotions. For example, baby blue is a very calming, peaceful color that makes us feel relaxed and safe, whereas magenta is a super fun color that gives us energy and leaves us feeling joyful.

Colors are an important part of your personal style aesthetic, especially in your personal spaces. If you have a bedroom with colors you don't enjoy or that make you feel stressed or hungry, you won't enjoy spending time there and will find it hard to have a restful sleep.

You can use Pinterest for inspiration on how you would like your personal space to look. From the colors that would suit each room best, to the pieces of decor that inspire you. Make the process fun and design how you would like your spaces to look. It doesn't have to be expensive; you can repurpose many of the things you already own and do other personal style things as a DIY project —you can even find some jewels in antique shops or garage sales.

Have fun with the redesigning process, take as much time as you need, and adopt the habit of keeping your space clean, organized, and clutter-free. You will be amazed at how much of an impact this change has on your life.

Part 4: How to Keep The Good Work Going

Hello, new you, or I should say real you! Thank you for taking this ride of healing yourself and discovering who you truly are.

At this stage, I imagine you feel lighter, happier, and more motivated than ever. You probably spend more time doing what you love, surround yourself with beautiful things that light you up and make you feel comfortable, have better relationships, and welcome new people in your life. Overall, you are a more authentic version of yourself.

Unfortunately, many people don't realize that our vibration or how we feel in a particular moment attracts other similar experiences, people, and situations. We are all energy; as such, we have a vibrational frequency.

When our thoughts, feelings, and intentions are negative, it affects our overall vibration, and we also attract negative experiences, people, and situations into our lives. That is why releasing negative habits, people, thoughts, and emotions significantly raises our vibration so that the things we attract into our lives are more positive.

If you have taken every step of this journey, you are also starting to attract more positivity into your life and a better future for yourself. Although life is not always positive, and there can be other negative experiences you need to face moving forward, this doesn't mean your vibration needs to change, or that it will be lower again. It means living a happier life, with inner peace and fulfillment, requires us to make conscious choices every day of our lives.

In this part of the book, I want to share some concepts, habits, and practices that can help you maintain your positive way of being and the results achieved from this program so far.

First, I want to acknowledge the power we all have as humans. We are extremely powerful beings, even though we sometimes don't realize that we have everything we need to change our reality, no matter how difficult it seems. I want you to feel empowered and confident that you don't have to go back to your old ways of living ever again and that you can create everything you want.

Then I will share some self-love and self-care tips that can help you continue developing a better relationship with yourself. When we feel unconditionally loved, there is no space for fear. We stop fearing rejection and abandonment because we provide ourselves with all the love we need. And from that space of fulfillment, we can also love others unconditionally. Having a self-love practice also allows us to build and maintain stronger relationships with others, relationships based on true, unconditional love.

After that, I will guide you through some habits that can help you keep some balance in your life. That is important because when we are balanced, we are more emotionally stable, physically healthier, and feel better. The stresses of everyday life can throw us out of balance, which is why maintaining healthy habits and acknowledging when it is time to regain balance in our lives is one of the keys to maintaining our inner peace and well-being.

Since being more spiritual, my life has substantially improved. That's why I wanted to share with you how I found my spiritual path and invite you to look for a spiritual practice that could suit you —if that interests you.

Your spiritual practice doesn't have to be religious or even esoteric. It can be as simple as connecting more with yourself, your true essence, and nature; it can be about being more mindful and present in the moment and living your life more consciously.

Finally, I will share the importance of living a life without clutter and why it is important to declutter our life regularly from physical objects and habits, thoughts, gadgets, social media, and other activities that accumulate with time and take up time, space, money and energy we could be using for something else that brings us true joy.

Understand Your Power

Most people have no idea how powerful we are as human beings. Mainstream education never teaches us that we can all change our external reality by changing our internal world, healing our wounds, and getting to know ourselves.

Thanks to this book, you have already started to experience how powerful you are. You know how you can change your life completely by letting go of everything that doesn't serve you and focusing on what you truly want.

When we understand our power, nothing can shake us again. Our power lies in our mind, in the things we focus on, and in the perspective with which we view things. There are always many sides to a situation; we can always choose to focus on the positive aspect instead of the negative.

For example, if we face rejection, we can choose to see it as universal protection to ensure that we don't build relationships with people misaligned with our highest good. If we lose our job, we can see that it was to open space for better opportunities to come into our lives. If a person says hurtful things, we can choose to see how this person is projecting her thoughts onto us the same way we do it with others.

Understanding our power helps us keep our inner peace even when facing adversity, problems, or change. It gives us the tools to rise above any situation, see it from a different perspective, learn the lesson if there is one and let it go. That way, we don't store negative feelings in our emotional bodies or let external circumstances influence our well-being. I first realized this when I started letting go of my feelings and attachment to the bullying I suffered.

As shared in my story, I was a victim of workplace bullying and harassment. My boss wanted me to leave the company and started to do horrible things to ridicule me and humiliate me in front of others. Many coworkers joined him and started treating me horribly too.

Because I was in a foreign country without speaking the language very well and without support, there was little I could do to defend myself. My husband was part of the process but didn't have the knowledge or support from others to know what to do.

At one time, I couldn't even leave the house because I was so afraid of facing those people and the public humiliation. So one day, I just prayed and hoped that God or the universe could hear me and help me escape the situation because I couldn't see how I could get out of it by myself. Soon after, I came across a video discussing the power of your mind and how what we focus on grows because we give a lot of energy to it. That video helped me understand that I was just giving it momentum by always thinking about the bullying.

I decided to test if that was true by doing my best to stop focusing on it. After I left that place, I focused on the things that were going well in my life, instead of thinking about the bullying.

Now, focusing on something else doesn't mean you should suppress or repress what is happening and how you are feeling. It means to let it be, accept how things turned out without the need to change them, and turn your awareness to something more positive.

When you accept the situation and shift your focus to the positive aspects around you, you are actually raising your vibration, which allows you to come to a successful resolution. This happens because you cannot solve an issue when you are in the same emotional state that got you there in the first place. To see the bigger picture, you need to rise above what is happening, and that is achieved through acceptance of what is.

After some time, I started noticing how my life situation improved; I didn't come across those people anymore and slowly started forgetting what had happened. My perspective on things also changed. For example, I stopped seeing the situation from a victim's point of view and realized that it was a lesson I needed to learn. What I had gone through reflected what was happening inside me. I didn't love and accept myself for who I was, didn't think I was enough, and couldn't see my worth. So the outer world was mirroring that back to me.

The other lesson was that the rejection I suffered was a detour so I could find my path. I remained stuck in a job I hated but didn't dare to change, although I knew I was meant for something else. I was around people who didn't love me genuinely and were either using me or bringing me down. When I understood this lesson, I could release the pain and forgive the people involved because it was clear to me that it had been a blessing in disguise. Without that experience, I would still be miserable at my job, without real friends, with severe social anxiety and low self-esteem, and without knowing who I truly am. A shift in perspective was how I regained my power and how you can do it, regardless of your situation.

From the moment I gained that deep understanding, my life started turning in a completely different direction, and I never again thought about that dark period of my life until I decided to write this book.

So I want to share this insight with you because even if you are consciously aware or not, your thoughts are creating your reality. When you experience a difficult or challenging situation, even if it is something small like a disagreement, I invite you to be in your power by not feeding energy into the negativity, letting go of the negative emotions, accepting what is, and choosing to focus on something else.

Create a Self-Care Self -Love Routine

Throughout this book, you have been on a self-discovery journey, especially from step 9, where you started questioning and genuinely contemplating your values, what you truly want in life, and what talents you have, among other aspects that make you uniquely you. Knowing our true selves allows us to be confident in what we can do and the decisions we make. It helps us stop caring about what others think of us and recognize our value and potential.

We are all valuable and come from the same source; that's why there is no such thing as an innately more important or less important person, especially not because of our money, career, fame, beauty, and other external things. We all have the same value and importance because we are all here for a reason and to serve a unique purpose. And we all have our unique talents and gifts. No one person in this world lacks a unique talent.

High self-esteem means we feel equal to others and just as capable as they are. If we think we are better than others, this normally shows that we don't value ourselves enough and need to inflate our ego to feel better about ourselves. This is a sign of low self-esteem and low self-worth. The same happens when we feel less than others.

Putting other people on a pedestal or thinking they are worthier because of money, status, fame, or other external reasons is detrimental because we do not see our value or the important role/part we all have to play.

When you know who you are, you realize your many talents and gifts and understand how you make a difference in this world by being you. And at that moment, you stop comparing yourself to others because it is clear you are not comparable since you are unique and have a unique purpose. The moment we stop comparing, expecting to be like someone else, or being jealous of others, we start valuing and loving ourselves for who we are.

Therefore, self-love is the most important thing you can give yourself and others. And this love doesn't come from an external source; it needs to come from you first. When we love and accept ourselves unconditionally, our cup is full, and we can love others from a place of unconditional love and for who they are without expecting anything in return. We don't sacrifice ourselves to receive love, admiration, or attention from others because we already have everything we need.

Self-love is also important for assertiveness and setting healthy boundaries with others.

During my journey, I realized that most of the difficult experiences in my teen and adult years were due to a lack of self-love and self-appreciation. I allowed so much abuse because I didn't think I deserved better and was worthy of love. When others bullied me, I didn't do anything because I felt I didn't have a voice. I kept false friends in my life because I thought it was ok for them to put me down and make me feel less than others.

The moment I started loving and accepting myself completely, with all my faults and weaknesses, with every bad decision I had made, I felt a deep appreciation for myself and couldn't understand how I had allowed all those things to happen.

From that day, I became assertive, confident, and good at setting healthy boundaries. I no longer allow mistreatment or sacrifice myself to gain external approval; my approval is the only thing that matters to me. More importantly, I don't allow people who don't love me and accept me for who I am into my life.

And self-love is not a one-time thing; it is a daily choice. It means allowing ourselves to pause when we feel stressed. It means nourishing our bodies, setting aside time for self-care, being patient with ourselves if something doesn't go as planned, and deciding to say no when someone asks us to do something we don't want to do. Setting boundaries and saying no is not a selfish act; it is an act of self-love because we are honoring and respecting our own needs.

My invitation to you is to continue choosing yourself every day. With every decision you make, honor your needs, dreams, and aspirations. Choose to take care of your body to keep it healthy because that allows you to have better mental and emotional health. And talk to yourself with loving kindness to stop negative self-talk.

I also encourage you to maintain a self-care practice. It doesn't have to be a daily or a very long routine. All you really have to do is to set aside personal time regularly to do something you love or check in with your feelings or goals. Self-love/care activities will vary from person to person, and you can choose anything you love to do.

In my case, I practice a daily self-care routine in the evening before going to bed by showering and caring for my skin. It is very simple, but it makes me relax and feel good about myself. I also take an hour on the weekends to do something I love. It doesn't have to be the same thing every time. Sometimes I like taking a long bath; other times, I go for a walk, cook something new, or read a book. It all depends on what I feel like doing or what I feel I need at the moment. If you have a specific thing you love doing, you could set a schedule to do it every other day or every week.

When you regularly spend time with yourself doing what you love, it deepens your connection with yourself. See it as a relationship you would have with another person. If you don't find time to nurture the relationship, you cannot build the intimacy of a partnership or deep friendship.

A self-care practice will also help you stay tuned to your needs and develop deeper intuition. When you know yourself, it is easier to identify what your internal guidance is calling you to do. When you listen to your intuition, you can make better decisions and follow a path aligned to achieving your purpose in life, leading to a happier and more fulfilling life.

For all those reasons, self-love is the most important concept you can take from this book moving forward. If you are in a place of deep self-love and appreciation, you will find it easier to relate to others and won't take anything they say or do personally. Your compassion and appreciation for yourself and others will grow, it will be easier to forgive; and, the best part: you will live a more abundant and fulfilling life.

Keep Working On Yourself

We never stop changing or learning more about ourselves. I believe part of our purpose in this life is to get to know who we truly are, peel the layers hiding our true selves, and show this self to the world.

For me, inner work is a lifetime process. Even the most enlightened person in the world has to keep working on themselves to get to higher levels of personal understanding and live through love, peace, and compassion.

Additionally, as part of our growth, we constantly face challenges that can throw us out of balance. Going within to solve those challenges and see what we can learn from the situation allows us to let it go without carrying additional baggage.

Keeping balance in our lives is the key to living an abundant and prosperous life. We need balance in our relationships, activities, health, emotions, routines, and everything we do.

To maintain balance in life, we must continue inner work and self-love practices. That means you must make the daily choice to think positive, live with integrity and release what is not serving you anymore.

Inner work is all about getting to know yourself better every day. It means finding what triggers you and solving the underlying issue causing your reactions. It is also about finding the behavioral patterns you have been carrying through your life, especially those that are sabotaging your success in different areas of life. Only then can you become more compassionate towards others and find your real purpose in this life.

Inner work connects you with your intuition, the part of you that is wise and has the answers you need to change your life. It allows you to develop a deeper level of confidence and unconditional love for yourself, thereby ensuring nothing and no one can manipulate your emotions again. When we listen to our intuition and act upon it, we make better decisions and follow the best path. We effortlessly flow through life and know that everything is how it should be, no matter what happens.

Understanding how your brain works and how you can rewire it to transform your life is essential to inner work. When you know how to access your subconscious mind and reprogram the inner narrative playing in the background, you can easily change limiting beliefs and negative thoughts to focus on what is important to you and attract positive experiences into your life.

As mentioned earlier, you can use this guideline as an inner work tool to continue the healing process layer by layer, get to know yourself on a deeper level, and release what you have accumulated and is now holding you back. You can come back to nurture your inner child, accept your shadow, and remind yourself how beautiful and powerful you are.

You can also look for other tools or practices that help you know yourself better. Therapy is an excellent way to discover parts of yourself you weren't aware of and change behavior patterns.

Working with a coach might help you understand what is blocking your success in different areas of your life. Taking a spiritual path can also reveal many tools and help you develop a deeper understanding of who you are and what you are here to do. Even something as simple as reading books and looking for resources that expand your consciousness and help you understand yourself better can help you reach your highest potential.

In this book's Appendix, I will list all the books that helped me on my journey. From psychology and personal development to spirituality and even novels, all those books contributed to my healing and have great concepts you can apply to your life.

Consider a Spiritual Practice

Since this could be a controversial topic, I was hesitant to include it in this book. However, I cannot lie about my healing journey, of which spirituality was an important part.

However, the essence of this strategy is not to impose anything on you; it is to leave the door open for anyone who wants to explore their spirituality a bit more deeply.

I see spirituality as any belief—religious or not—that helps you connect to a divine source, the universe, or a higher intelligence, whatever that may be. But most importantly, a path that connects you with yourself.

Since we are all spirits and have a soul, we are all innately spiritual.

Having a spiritual practice doesn't mean following a religion or ideal. It can simply be about understanding yourself as divine and connecting with that part of yourself that is wise. It can also be about your connection with nature, plants, and animals. Like my case, it can also be about seeking knowledge and truth.

I grew up in a catholic family, but my parents did not believe in anything, so I always had those contradictory concepts during my childhood. But since I can remember, I would ask myself how everything could be so perfect: our bodies, minds, and nature are complex and perfect systems that work without us consciously doing anything. I was amazed by how we are all connected in one way or another, and everything unfolds at the perfect time.

I decided to look for answers when I was at my lowest and darkest point. I felt like I needed the motivation to continue and wanted to find my real purpose in this life if I was to get out of my depression. That led me to start the process of seeking the truth, questioning every concept, and finding what resonates with me the most. I now follow a personal spiritual practice consisting of concepts I believe to be true.

What my spiritual path brought into my life was inner peace and the knowledge that everything was and is happening for me and not to me. It has allowed me to accept that I am not the victim of my circumstances and have the power to change them if I set my mind to doing so. It made me feel connected with myself and others and gave me a sense of security that everything is happening for a reason and in perfect timing.

A spiritual practice can be anything that makes you feel connected with everything and everyone, realize your potential and feel safe and protected. When we release the need to control everything around us and understand there is a higher force in the universe helping us learn the lessons we came here to learn and fulfill our purpose, we can flow in life and stop worrying so much about the future, because we know that everything will be fine.

As a child, my family's religious beliefs didn't really answer my questions about life and the universe. It made me feel faulty and unworthy of unconditional love. When I discovered that I am a divine being and part of something bigger and that God, the universe, the divine consciousness, or whatever you would like to call it, was always helping me be the best version of myself, I understood that everything is happening at the perfect time for me and there was nothing else I should be doing. I learned that every situation brings a lesson we can learn and helps us grow. And above all, we are not alone in this journey.

On my path to self-betterment and transformation, I use meditation and walking in nature as my spiritual practices. Meditation leaves me feeling connected to the divine, the cosmos, and my soul. It helps me listen to my intuition more and receive guidance from the part of me that is wise.

We rarely listen to our intuition, and sometimes we do the opposite; the world encourages us not to listen to what we feel or what our internal guidance is telling us. Although logic and reason are very important in our human experience, our intuition is equally important because our divine guidance helps us make decisions aligned with our true purpose in life.

Walking in nature helps me connect with all people, plants, and animals on the planet. It makes me feel grounded, safe, and like I am part of everything and we are all one. Nature also helps me release stress and negative emotions and transform them into peaceful energy. And makes me feel rejuvenated and joyful.

No matter what spiritual practices you feel drawn to, I recommend choosing at least one that helps you feel connected, safe, and protected. When we gain this confidence, we feel more empowered to go after what we want and stop overthinking or worrying about the future, which gives us the inner peace we seek.

Keep Your Life Clutter Free

In Part 2 of the book, you went through a deep decluttering process of everything that wasn't serving you anymore. You are now lighter, baggage-free, and well-positioned to enjoy the beauty surrounding you in your personal spaces. However, the decluttering process is a continuous process, not a one-time thing.

With time, you might realize that you have started accumulating more things, gotten distracted by things and activities you don't really enjoy, or have new relationships that are not helping you grow. You might also identify new negative beliefs that keep you stuck or block your success. This is all normal.

In life, we all go through ups and downs and have more stressful times when we stop focusing on ourselves and our well-being because we are busy solving the problems that life throws at us.

When you start feeling stuck in life, overwhelmed with everything you need to do, or simply don't feel motivated anymore, I invite you to start the decluttering process again. Getting rid of the things that no longer serve us at any given point frees up time and space, allowing us to focus on what we want to do.

You can also create a decluttering routine for material things. Having a good home declutter at least once a year can help you maintain your space tidy and curated, so you can always feel comfortable there. It can also help you understand how you have changed and your new personal style.

I also recommend periodically doing a digital declutter of all your gadgets, social media following, subscriptions, newsletters, and apps. It is astonishing how much digital clutter we accumulate, often of things that no longer interest us and are just distractors in our lives.

You might not see how this can affect you, but let me tell you that every time you get an email about something you don't care about, it clutters your email inbox and robs you of time and mental energy you could have spent doing something else.

It is also important to let go of negative thoughts, beliefs, and emotions. In this case, there is no specific time frame. I would only recommend being aware of the people and situations that trigger you and make you feel frustrated, angry, or sad. If someone or something triggers, there is probably an unresolved issue that you need to address and heal. Doing the healing work when the trigger occurs allows you to stop carrying negative emotions and thoughts, ensuring they don't accumulate again.

The same is true for negative relationships. Even if you have developed assertiveness and healthy boundaries that keep you away from toxic people, there is always the chance that you might meet someone who doesn't have the best intention or is simply not a match for you.

Keeping your life clutter free will help you focus on building the life you want and achieving your goals. It will help you release the heaviness and feel light again. Most importantly, it will free up time and space so new, better things can come into your life.

Conclusion

Thank you for embarking in this journey with me. Let me just take some time to tell you how proud of you I am for coming this far.

The inner work you have done through this book hasn't been easy. It doesn't only take courage but also commitment to face everything we don't want to face like our fears, shadows and deep rooted pain. It takes great courage to leave our comfort zone. And you have done it!

You saw yourself in a different light, found what obstacles were hindering your success and took action to remove them. You took time to get to know yourself better and accept all parts of you unconditionally. And most importantly, you took steps to build the life you truly want to live.

So please be proud of yourself and use this time to acknowledge and celebrate how far you have come.

Now let me remind you that all the tools you have learned throughout this process are always there for you to help you navigate new challenges that life might throw at you in the future. You can always come back to the different sections and start the process all over again.

The practices you have learned can go with you for the rest of your life. You can now heal faster by letting go of emotions as soon as they arise, by being more conscious of your behaviours and by focusing on positive outcomes instead of negative ones. You can also reprogram your mind so you start attracting everything you want to achieve in your life.

And remember, healing is a journey. All these steps you have gone through have most certainly transformed you but it doesn't mean that it is the end of inner work. Instead, choose to consciously work towards your healing everyday. Release negative emotions when they arise so you don't have to carry them with you. Acknowledge your shadow aspects when you react instinctively. And always take care of your needs and choose yourself first.

I won't lie, since I finished my healing process I have had difficult experiences again. I have temporarily lost faith and I have fallen back into negative habits and limiting beliefs. And that is ok too. But as soon as I realize that I might be off track I remind myself to go back to my healing techniques, and I start the process all over again. And that is what I invite you to do as well.

So now enjoy the beginning of your new life, a more conscious life. The amount of inner work you have done has shifted your consciousness into a different state, where you are more compassionate towards yourself and others, you see the positive things in life and live your life more authentically. This will bring new positive people and things into your life.

And never forget: you are a powerful being. You can achieve anything you set your mind to. You have a unique set of characteristics that make you perfect just the way your are. So don't hesitate any longer, go after your dreams and start building the life you truly want to live.

Appendix

This is a list of the books and other resources that inspired me through my journey or that I refer to in some parts of the book.

Byrne, R. (2006). The Secret. New York: Atria Books.

Campbell, R. (2015). Light Is the New Black: A Guide To Answering Your Soul'S Callings And Working Your Light. London, Hay House UK Ltd.

Hawkins, David R. M. D. Ph. D. (2012). Letting Go: The Pathway of Surrender, Paperback. [United States], Hay House, Inc.

Hendricks, G. (20102009). The big leap: conquer your hidden fear and take life to the next level (1st HarperCollins pbk. ed.). [United States], HarperCollins.

Kahn, M. (2021). The Universe Always Has a Plan: The 10 Golden Rules of Letting Go. [United States], Hay House Inc.

Kondō, M., & Zeller, E. W. (2015). The life-changing magic of tidying up: the Japanese art of decluttering and organizing. Unabridged. [United States], Tantor Media, Inc.

Korb, A. (2015). The upward spiral: Using neuroscience to reverse the course of depression, one small change at a time. [United States], New Harbinger Publications.

Robbins, M. (2017). The 5 Second Rule: Transform Your Life, Work, and Confidence with Everyday Courage . [United States], Post Hill Press.

Shetty, J. (2020). Think like a monk: train your mind for peace and purpose every day. New York, Simon & Schuster.

Singer, M. A. (2007). The untethered soul: The journey beyond yourself. New Harbinger Publications.

Tipping, C. (2010). Radical Forgiveness: A Revolutionary Five-Stage Process to: Heal Relationships - Let Go of Anger and Blame - Find Peace. [United States], Sounds True.

Tolle, E. (2001). The power of now. [England], Hodder Paperback.

Table of Contents